The Book On

Taking Flight

Mastering The Skies in Private Pilot Training

The Book On Series

Quinn Hartley

Published by The Book On Publishing, 2025.

First edition. October 19, 2025

Website: https://thebookon.ca

Substack: https://thebookonpublishing.substack.com/

The Book On Taking Flight: Mastering the Skies in Private Pilot Training
First edition. October 19, 2025

ISBN: 978-1-997909-39-2

Written by Quinn Hartley

The Book On Series

The Book On Life Unscripted
The Book On Risk Management in Payments
The Book On AI for Everyday People
The Book On Relationships
The Book On Master The Algorithm
The Book On Saying No
The Book On Community-Led Strategy
The Book On The Myth of Multitasking
The Book On The Burnout Blueprint
The Book On The Digital Reboot
The Book On The Shape of What's Coming
The Book On Strategic Obsession
The Book On High-Stakes Thinking
The Book On Artificial Leverage
The Book On Clarity
The Book On Uncertainty
The Book On Operational Excellence
The Book On Escape
The Book On Reinvention After Consequences
The Book On Re-Unifying Society
The Book On Taking Flight
The Book On Persuasion
The Book On Enough
The Book On Attention
The Book On Men (for Women)
The Book On Women (for Men)
The Book On The Cookbook for Cannibals

Who This Book Is For

This book is for the dreamers.

For anyone who's ever looked up as a small plane passed overhead and thought, *Could I really do that?* For those who've felt a pull—not just toward the sky, but toward something bigger, something freer.

Maybe you've always loved airplanes but never leaped. Perhaps you've assumed flying is only for the military, the wealthy, or some elite club. Perhaps part of you wants this, but another part says, *Not me. Not yet.*

This book is your permission slip. It's your walk around the cockpit before you ever set foot in it.

You don't need to have signed up for flight school. You don't need to know what "VFR," "trim," or "ATC" stand for.

All you need is the curiosity to ask: *What would it feel like to sit in the left seat and take off under your own command?*

Inside, you'll find a mix of real stories, plainspoken guidance, and grounded wisdom—from someone who's made the journey and wants you to know: You can too.

This is not a textbook. It's a takeoff checklist for your curiosity. No pressure. Just possibilities.

Ready to find out what flight might mean for you?

Table Of Contents

Chapter 1: Taking Flight: A Journey Begins

The moment begins with a dream, a vision etched against an endless sky. For some, it arrives suddenly during a chance encounter with a small aircraft gracefully banking over a summer landscape, its wings catching the golden afternoon light. For others, it builds slowly, a persistent whisper that grows stronger with each commercial flight taken as a passenger, each airshow attended, each documentary watched. This dream—the desire to become a pilot—represents one of humanity's most enduring aspirations, a tangible connection to the ancient longing to slip the surly bonds of Earth and touch the face of the heavens. What sets private pilot training apart from mere fantasy is the remarkable accessibility of this dream in our modern era. Unlike the early pioneers of aviation who risked life and limb in fragile contraptions of wood and canvas, today's aspiring pilot enters a well-established world of certified instruction, proven training methodologies, and reliable aircraft. Yet the magic remains undiminished. The transformation from earthbound dreamer to certified private pilot represents a profound personal journey that challenges not only your technical abilities but also your discipline, judgment, and character. This journey begins not in the cockpit, but in the mind, with the conscious decision to commit to a path that will forever change how you perceive the world around you.

Understanding what motivates you to pursue private pilot training provides essential insight into the journey ahead. Some arrive at the flight school driven by practical considerations, the ability to travel efficiently for business, reach remote properties, or reduce travel time between destinations. These pragmatic pilots often prove among the most diligent students, recognizing that mastery of aviation skills serves concrete life goals. Others seek the pure joy of flight itself, the visceral thrill of maneuvering in three-dimensional space, the incomparable freedom of commanding your own aircraft. These passion-driven students bring infectious enthusiasm to their training, though they sometimes must learn to temper excitement with the methodical discipline that aviation demands. Still others come to flying through family tradition, following in the contrails of parents or grandparents who flew, honoring a legacy while creating their own relationship with flight. Then some arrive at aviation later in life, having deferred their dream through decades of other responsibilities, and now finally claim time for themselves. Each motivation carries its own strengths and challenges, but all valid paths converge at the same destination: the fundamental knowledge and skills required to operate an aircraft safely. Recognizing your personal motivation helps sustain commitment through the inevitable challenges ahead, providing a touchstone to return to when training becomes demanding or progress feels slow.

The decision to pursue private pilot certification carries significant implications that extend far beyond simply learning to fly an airplane. You are entering a community with its own culture, language, and traditions, becoming part of an international fellowship bound by shared knowledge and mutual respect for the sky. This community traces its lineage back to the Wright brothers and encompasses everyone from weekend recreational pilots to airline captains, from aerobatic performers to bush pilots operating in remote wilderness. Within this diverse family of aviators, the private pilot certificate serves as your entry credential, proof that you have mastered the fundamental competencies required to participate safely. The training process itself will reshape how you think, teaching systematic problem-solving, precise communication, spatial reasoning, and risk management in ways that prove valuable far beyond aviation. Students often report that learning to fly enhances their performance in entirely unrelated fields, sharpening decision-making abilities and building confidence through the mastery of genuinely complex skills. The certificate you eventually earn opens doors to experiences unavailable through any other means, flying yourself to destinations that would take hours by car, viewing landscapes from perspectives that photographs can never fully capture, and sharing the gift of flight with friends and family. These experiences accumulate into something profound, a fundamental shift in your relationship with geography, weather, and the natural world.

Before beginning formal training, prospective students invariably confront questions about feasibility, both personal and practical. The most common concern centers on aptitude: Do I have what it takes to learn to fly? This question reflects understandable uncertainty, particularly among those without technical backgrounds or mechanical experience. The reassuring truth, supported by decades of flight training data, reveals that successful pilots emerge from every conceivable background and educational level. While specific abilities prove helpful — such as reasonable hand-eye coordination, capacity for focused attention, and basic mathematical literacy — none require exceptional talent. Flying skills develop through practice and repetition, not innate genius. The average person has the skills needed to become a proficient private pilot. What matters far more than natural aptitude is consistency of effort, willingness to study, openness to feedback, and persistence through learning plateaus. Students with limited technical backgrounds often succeed admirably by approaching training with methodical dedication. At the same time, those with extensive engineering or aviation knowledge sometimes struggle if they over-intellectualize tasks that require physical practice and muscle memory. Age similarly proves less determinative than commonly assumed. While younger students may adapt more quickly to certain physical aspects of aircraft control, older students often excel in judgment and decision-making, bringing life experience that enhances situational awareness. Students have successfully earned private pilot certificates from their teenage years through their seventies and beyond, each age group bringing distinct advantages to the training process.

Financial considerations represent another critical dimension of the decision to pursue pilot training, deserving careful examination and realistic planning. Private pilot training requires a meaningful investment, with total costs typically ranging from 8,000 to 15,000 dollars, depending on geographic location, aircraft rental rates, and individual learning pace. This figure encompasses flight instruction time, ground instruction, aircraft rental, training materials, medical examination fees, knowledge test and practical test expenses, and various miscellaneous costs that accumulate throughout training. The investment extends beyond money to include a substantial time commitment; most students require forty to seventy hours of flight training, plus considerable additional hours devoted to ground study, pre-flight preparation, and post-flight debriefing. For working professionals, parents, or students balancing other commitments, allocating sufficient time can pose a greater challenge than funding the training itself. However, understanding these requirements upfront enables realistic planning that dramatically improves training success rates. Students who attempt training without adequate time or financial resources often experience frustration, extended training timelines, and, at times, abandonment of the goal altogether. Those who enter training with a clear understanding of required commitments, established budgets, and dedicated time blocks tend to progress steadily toward certification. The investment ultimately purchases not just a certificate but a skill set that lasts a lifetime, opening possibilities that remain available throughout your years, making the cost remarkably reasonable when viewed across decades of potential flying enjoyment.

The medical certification process represents your first formal interaction with aviation's regulatory framework, introducing you to standards that govern all aspects of flying. The Federal Aviation Administration requires private pilot applicants to obtain at a minimum a third-class medical certificate, issued by an Aviation Medical Examiner after examination confirming you meet basic health standards. This examination evaluates vision, hearing, cardiovascular health, neurological function, and mental health, ensuring that pilots are physically and psychologically fit to operate aircraft safely. For most healthy individuals, obtaining a medical certificate is straightforward —a routine examination that identifies any issues requiring special attention. However, certain medical conditions or medication use may complicate certification, requiring additional documentation or special issuance procedures. Prospective students with known health concerns, including conditions like diabetes, previous cardiac events, attention deficit disorders, or depression requiring medication, should consult with an Aviation Medical Examiner before beginning expensive flight training, ensuring certification remains possible before investing substantially. The medical certification process also introduces the concept of pilot responsibility that permeates all aspects of aviation. Pilots must self-assess fitness for each flight, grounding themselves when illness, medication, fatigue, or stress might compromise safety. This culture of personal responsibility, backed by regulatory requirements but ultimately dependent on individual integrity, is a fundamental aspect of aviation safety. Learning to evaluate your capabilities and limitations honestly begins with the medical certification process and continues throughout your flying career.

Selecting the right flight school and instructor constitutes one of your most essential decisions in the journey toward certification. The relationship between student and instructor profoundly influences not only the efficiency of your training but also your development as a safe, competent pilot and your long-term enjoyment of aviation. Flight schools range from large, well-established operations with multiple aircraft and instructors to independent instructors operating at smaller airports. Each model offers distinct advantages. Larger schools typically provide structured curricula, scheduling flexibility, backup aircraft and instructors, and comprehensive resources including simulators, briefing rooms, and administrative support. These institutions often prove ideal for students who value consistency and predictability. Smaller operations or independent instructors frequently offer more personalized attention, flexible approaches tailored to individual learning styles, and often more affordable rates. The best choice depends on your learning preferences, schedule requirements, and local options. When evaluating schools, consider factors beyond cost alone. Examine aircraft condition and maintenance quality; your life depends on airworthiness. Observe instructor-student interactions to assess whether the teaching style aligns with how you learn best. Inquire about completion rates and average time-to-certificate, indicators of program effectiveness. Visit the facility and note whether the environment feels professional, welcoming, and organized. Trust your instincts about cultural fit; you will spend substantial time in this environment, and comfort level affects learning efficiency.

The instructor you select, or who is assigned to you, becomes your guide through the intricate process of learning to fly, making this relationship among the most influential in your aviation journey. An excellent flight instructor combines technical knowledge, teaching ability, patience, and genuine investment in student success. Technical proficiency alone does not guarantee effective instruction; the best instructors excel at breaking complex tasks into manageable components, explaining concepts in multiple ways to accommodate different learning styles, and recognizing when students need encouragement rather than frank assessment of areas needing improvement. During your first interactions with a potential instructor, evaluate communication style and teaching philosophy. Do explanations make sense to you? Does the instructor listen attentively to your questions and concerns? Do you feel respected and valued, or merely processed through a standardized program? Chemistry matters enormously in the instructor-student relationship. Training will include moments of stress, frustration, and challenge; facing these moments with an instructor you trust and respect makes them surmountable, while personality conflicts can transform everyday training difficulties into insurmountable obstacles. Remember that you are the customer, and changing instructors remains an option if the relationship proves unproductive. While changing instructors may slightly extend training time as the new instructor assesses your skills, a compatible instructor relationship ultimately accelerates progress. Some students even benefit from occasionally flying with multiple instructors, gaining exposure to different perspectives and techniques that enrich overall learning.

Your earliest experiences at the airport and around aircraft mark the beginning of your practical education, introducing you to an environment that will become intimately familiar. The airport itself operates as a small city with its own rules, customs, and infrastructure. The flight line, where aircraft are parked, bustles with activity: planes taxiing to and from runways, mechanics performing maintenance, pilots conducting preflight inspections, and fuel trucks servicing aircraft. Learning to navigate this environment safely requires attention to specific hazards: spinning propellers that can be instantly fatal, hot exhaust from running engines, wingtips protruding into walkways, and fuel spills that create slipping hazards. Your instructor will teach proper procedures for approaching and moving around aircraft, as well as situational awareness techniques that become second nature with practice. The ramp environment demands constant vigilance but also offers the excitement of being surrounded by diverse aircraft, each representing different capabilities and missions. You will learn to identify common aircraft types by sight, understanding how a sleek Cirrus differs from a sturdy Cessna, recognizing vintage aircraft alongside modern glass-cockpit models. This education extends to airport facilities, the flight planning room where pilots review weather and file flight plans, the pilot lounge where aviators gather to share stories and advice, and the maintenance hangars where the detailed work of keeping aircraft airworthy occurs behind the scenes. Becoming comfortable in this environment, understanding its rhythms and protocols, represents an essential early milestone in your transformation from visitor to participant in the aviation community.

The aircraft itself —most likely a small, single-engine trainer such as a Cessna 172 or Piper Cherokee —will become the most significant tool in your education, and understanding its systems will lay the foundation for all practical flying skills. Your early interactions with the aircraft focus on familiarity and respect, learning its components and their functions before attempting to command its movement through the air. The preflight inspection, a systematic external and internal examination performed before every flight, becomes your first hands-on aviation skill. Under your instructor's guidance, you will learn to check fuel quantity and quality, ensuring no water contamination threatens engine operation. You will examine control surfaces —aileron (which banks the aircraft), elevator (which controls pitch), and rudder (which coordinates turns)—and verify that they move freely and correctly. You will inspect the propeller for nicks or damage that might cause dangerous vibration. You will ascertain that antennas, lights, and static ports remain secure and unobstructed. This process teaches attention to detail and systematic thinking while building a mechanical understanding of how the aircraft functions. Inside the cockpit, initial encounters with the instrument panel can feel overwhelming. Gauges, switches, radios, and indicators crowd the panel in seemingly chaotic profusion. Your instructor will methodically explain each instrument's purpose, how to interpret its indications, and which instruments matter most at different phases of flight. Modern training aircraft may feature advanced glass cockpit displays that present information digitally, or traditional analog instruments with mechanical gauges. Both systems provide the same essential information —airspeed, altitude, heading, engine performance, and navigation data — just packaged differently. Learning to scan these instruments efficiently while maintaining awareness outside the aircraft represents a core skill developed throughout training.

The first time you actually take the controls of an aircraft in flight remains etched in every pilot's memory, a moment of magic mixed with concentration so intense that time seems to compress. Most instructors plan the first lesson to include actual flight experience, understanding that handling the aircraft provides motivation and context for all the study and preparation that follows. After your instructor completes the takeoff, a task requiring coordination and precision that you will eventually master but that remains beyond reach during initial lessons, the aircraft climbs away from the airport, and your instructor speaks the words every student dreams of hearing: "You have the controls." Your hands settle onto the yoke, feeling the subtle pressures that convey the aircraft's response to airflow over its surfaces. Your feet rest on the rudder pedals, discovering how gentle pressure coordinates with turns. The instructor demonstrates how slight movements produce significant effects, how the aircraft responds to your inputs with willing sensitivity. You experiment with gentle turns, feeling the aircraft bank as you rotate the yoke, learning the unfamiliar sensation of controlling movement in three dimensions. The world below —roads, buildings, fields, trees — scrolls past in a perspective utterly unlike any ground experience or commercial airline flight. This is different, immediate, intimate. You are not a passenger; you are a pilot. The flight might last only an hour, and you may control the aircraft for only a fraction of that time, but something fundamental has shifted. The dream has become tangible. The journey is underway.

Returning from that first flight, even before the wheels touch back onto the runway, your mind begins processing the experience, sorting sensations and impressions into categories that will gradually organize into systematic knowledge. The physical sensations of flight, the G-forces during turns, the subtle vibrations transmitted through the airframe, the engine sounds at different power settings, start building a sensory vocabulary that will expand with every flight. Your instructor will debrief the lesson, discussing what went well and what needs practice, beginning the cyclical process of flying, analyzing, and improving that characterizes practical training. You will likely feel simultaneously exhilarated and exhausted, the mental workload of processing entirely new experiences demanding more energy than expected. This exhaustion is usual, a sign of genuine learning and neural pathway formation as your brain integrates novel information. In the days following your first flight, reflection continues. You may find yourself mentally replaying sequences, reviewing what the instructor explained, and researching topics that arose during the flight. This cognitive processing between flights proves nearly as valuable as flight time itself, consolidating learning and preparing your mind for subsequent lessons. The relationship between flight experience and ground study creates a synergistic learning cycle where each reinforces the other. Concepts studied theoretically make immediate sense when experienced in flight, while flight experiences motivate deeper study to understand the principles underlying what you observed.

As you stand at the beginning of this journey toward becoming a private pilot, the path ahead stretches through challenging terrain but toward a destination of immense personal significance. The coming chapters will explore every dimension of this training process, from mastering basic aircraft control to navigating cross-country flights, from understanding complex aerodynamics to managing emergencies, from communicating effectively with air traffic control to making sound aeronautical decisions under pressure. Each lesson builds upon previous learning, creating a progressive framework that transforms the seemingly impossible into the achievable. The journey demands patience with yourself during inevitable struggles, celebration of incremental victories that mark progress, and sustained commitment even when advancement feels slow. Some days flying will come easily, the aircraft responding to your touch as though reading your intentions. Other days will test your resolve as skills that seemed mastered suddenly elude you, as weather disrupts schedules, as fatigue or distraction interferes with performance. These variations represent normal aspects of learning any complex skill, particularly one as demanding as aviation. The students who succeed are not those who never struggle but those who persist through struggles, who learn from mistakes rather than being discouraged by them, who trust the training process even when immediate results disappoint. Your journey has begun with that first flight, that first moment of taking control and feeling an aircraft respond to your command. Everything that follows expands upon that foundational experience, deepening your skills and knowledge until the day when an FAA examiner shakes your hand and declares you qualified as a private pilot. That day will arrive not through magic but through dedicated effort, lesson by lesson, flight by flight, building the competence that makes dreams a reality and transforms skyward aspirations into earned wings.

Chapter 2: The Language of the Skies

The radio crackles to life in your headset, and you hear a stream of words that sound like English but feel entirely foreign: "November-Two-Three-Four-Five-Bravo, turn right heading zero-niner-zero, descend and maintain three thousand, altimeter two-niner-niner-two." Your instructor responds with practiced ease, the syllables flowing as naturally as ordinary conversation, and you realize with a mixture of excitement and intimidation that you're about to learn an entirely new language. Aviation communication represents far more than mere words exchanged between pilots and controllers; it forms the essential fabric that keeps thousands of aircraft safely separated in shared airspace, enables complex operations to unfold with precision, and transforms the chaotic potential of the sky into an ordered, predictable environment where everyone speaks with clarity, brevity, and purpose. This language didn't emerge overnight but evolved through decades of refinement, shaped by accidents that taught harsh lessons about the consequences of miscommunication and gradually standardized into the system we use today. Learning to speak like a pilot means understanding not just the words themselves but the philosophy behind them, the recognition that every syllable transmitted occupies valuable frequency space that dozens or even hundreds of other pilots might need, that ambiguity can kill, and that professional communication forms as crucial a skill as controlling the aircraft itself. The journey from nervous first transmission to confident radio work parallels your development as a pilot, reflecting growing competence, situational awareness, and the ability to anticipate the airplane while maintaining the mental bandwidth to communicate effectively.

Understanding the phonetic alphabet forms your first step into this linguistic world, though its importance extends far beyond simply knowing that Alpha means A and Bravo means B. The International Civil Aviation Organization phonetic alphabet exists because ordinary letter sounds often blur together, particularly through scratchy radios, with wind noise in the background, and when speakers have different accents or native languages. Try distinguishing between "M" and "N" in a garbled transmission at a critical moment, and you'll immediately appreciate why "Mike" and "November" provide unmistakable clarity. Your aircraft's registration number becomes your call sign, your unique identifier in the sky, and you'll use it so frequently that the phonetic rendering will eventually flow more naturally than the actual letters. An aircraft registered as N12345B isn't referred to by those raw characters in radio communication; it becomes "November-One-Two-Three-Four-Five-Bravo," and eventually, once you've established contact, controllers will shorten it to "Three-Four-Five-Bravo" or sometimes just "Five-Bravo" when there's no possibility of confusion. This system of progressive abbreviation reflects one of aviation communication's core principles: efficiency without sacrificing clarity. You learn to speak your call sign with distinct separation between elements, avoiding the common student mistake of running numbers together into an indistinct blur that forces controllers to ask for repeats, clogging up the frequency and revealing your inexperience. Each phonetic word should emerge clearly, with slight pauses that allow the listener's brain to process and retain the information. You'll discover that speaking slowly actually conveys professionalism, while speaking too quickly suggests nervousness and often requires repetition, ultimately taking more time than a measured initial delivery.

Numbers in aviation communication follow their own special rules, creating another layer in this language that seems designed to eliminate every possible ambiguity. Instead of saying "nine," pilots say "niner," a modification born from recognition that the standard pronunciation of nine sounds dangerously similar to the German word "nein," meaning no, potentially creating confusion in international operations. The number five becomes "fife" to distinguish it from "fire," which might otherwise sound alarmingly similar in emergency communications. Three becomes "tree" to prevent it from being mistaken for other numbers. These modifications feel awkward at first — self-conscious and theatrical — but they represent hard-won wisdom encoded in standard procedure. Altitude is communicated in specific ways depending on the context: below 18,000 feet, you speak each digit individually, so 3,500 feet becomes "three thousand five hundred." In contrast, above the transition altitude, where you switch to flight levels, altitudes are expressed differently. Flight Level Two Four Zero means twenty-four thousand feet, spoken with the assumption that pilots understand the convention. Headings follow their own protocol: always stated as three digits, meaning heading ninety degrees becomes "heading zero-niner-zero," ensuring no confusion between, say, heading ninety and heading nine. This redundancy serves a purpose; the extra digit provides a mental checkpoint that confirms you're discussing headings rather than altitudes or frequencies. Wind information follows a consistent pattern: direction, then speed, with direction given in magnetic north and always in three digits. Hence, a wind from two hundred degrees at fifteen knots becomes "wind two-zero-zero at one-five." The pattern repeats endlessly across all aviation communication: establish a standard format, maintain consistency, and eliminate variables that might confuse.

Radio frequencies themselves constitute another vocabulary entirely, a progression of numbers that unlock different services as you move through the aviation system. You'll start with your local tower frequency, probably something like 118.3 or 119.7 megahertz, though pilots never say "megahertz"; it's understood that all these frequencies operate in the VHF aviation band. When speaking frequencies, you maintain clarity by stating each digit clearly: "one-one-eight-point-three" for 118.3, never "one eighteen point three" which might blur together and cause confusion. Ground control occupies a different frequency, typically close to but distinct from tower, allowing controllers to manage the airspace with clear separation of responsibilities. Departure and approach control frequencies extend your communication range beyond the immediate airport environment, connecting you to radar controllers who manage the complex choreography of aircraft climbing out after takeoff or descending for landing. Flight service stations provide weather briefings and flight plan services, accessible via dedicated frequencies and remote communication outlets scattered across the country. As you gain experience, you'll accumulate a mental library of frequencies for your regular airports, the numbers becoming as familiar as phone numbers of close friends, automatically recalled when needed. The chart supplement, formerly called the Airport/Facility Directory, lists every frequency you might need, organized by airport and service type. Learning to extract the correct frequency from this dense resource quickly is another essential skill. Many students initially struggle with frequency management, forgetting to switch at the appropriate time or dialing in the wrong numbers under pressure, but this too becomes automatic with practice, part of the flowing sequence of actions that define competent flying.

The structure of radio transmissions follows a formula as rigid as any mathematical equation, though unlike mathematics, this formula exists not for abstract elegance but for immediate, practical clarity. Every transmission contains specific elements in a particular order: who you're calling, who you are, where you are, what you want, and what information you've received that affects your intentions. This might not sound very easy initially, but it creates a predictable pattern that allows controllers to quickly extract essential information from your transmission without needing to ask clarifying questions. Consider a typical initial call to a control tower: "Centerville Tower, Cherokee Two-Three-Four-Five-Bravo, ten miles south, inbound for landing, with information Alpha." In those few words, you've identified the facility you're calling, identified yourself completely, told them your position and distance, stated your intentions, and confirmed you have the current airport information, everything they need to integrate you into the traffic pattern and provide appropriate instructions. Compare this to a typical student mistake: "Uh, Centerville, this is a Cherokee, and we're, um, coming in to land?" The vague location, missing tail number, uncertain delivery, and question-like intonation all signal inexperience and force the controller to ask multiple follow-up questions, consuming precious frequency time and potentially delaying your integration into the traffic flow. Controllers aren't being pedantic when they insist on proper format; they're managing a dynamic three-dimensional puzzle where every piece of information must be precise and immediately usable. Your transmissions should sound like statements, not questions, delivered with confidence, even when you're internally uncertain, Fake it until you make it actually applies quite literally to radio work, as a professionally delivered transmission often prompts a more precise, more helpful response from controllers.

Reading back instructions forms one of aviation communication's most critical safety elements, creating a closed loop that verifies information was received correctly and understood as intended. When a controller issues a clearance or instruction, you don't simply acknowledge with "roger" and proceed; you read back the critical elements in your own words to confirm the shared understanding. "November-Four-Five-Bravo, turn right heading three-three-zero, descend and maintain four thousand five hundred" requires a readback: "Right three-three-zero, down to four thousand five hundred, Four-Five-Bravo." Notice that the readback uses slightly different words while preserving the essential information—the heading, the altitude, and your shortened call sign—which is now acceptable since you're in an established communication relationship with this controller. If you read back incorrect information, the controller will immediately correct you: "November-Four-Five-Bravo, negative, maintain five thousand five hundred," giving you the chance to fix the error before it becomes a dangerous deviation. This system catches an enormous number of potential mistakes — both pilot errors in hearing and controller errors in speaking — creating redundancy that keeps operations safe. Certain items always require readback: runway assignments, altitude assignments, heading assignments, airspeed restrictions, hold-short instructions, and any clearance to enter, cross, or land on a runway. The phrase "read back correct" from a controller confirms they've heard your readback and verified its accuracy, closing the communication loop. Students often struggle with the cognitive load of flying the airplane while simultaneously processing, remembering, and reading back instructions. Still, this skill develops with practice until you can write complex instructions on your kneeboard, read them back accurately, and begin executing them, all while maintaining aircraft control and situational awareness —a testament to the brain's remarkable ability to develop parallel-processing skills through training.

Airport operations introduce their own specialized vocabulary, a collection of terms that describe the various phases of flight from engine start to shutdown. The phrase "taxi to parking" means something quite different from "taxi to runway two-seven via alpha, bravo," and understanding these distinctions prevents you from inadvertently taking actions that could create dangerous situations. Ground control, which manages all aircraft movement on the airport surface except for the active runways, speaks a language of taxiways, hold-short lines, and progressive taxi instructions. When you request a taxi, you'll typically specify your intended flight direction or your destination airport, allowing controllers to assign an appropriate departure runway: "Ground, Cherokee Four-Five-Bravo, at the ramp with Bravo, taxi for departure to the south." The controller responds with taxi instructions that might seem simple, "Cherokee Four-Five-Bravo, taxi to runway three-six via taxiway alpha, hold short of runway two-seven", but contain critical safety information. That hold-short instruction requires a specific acknowledgment; you must read back the runway you're instructed to hold short of, creating a moment of forced attention that prevents runway incursions —one of aviation's most persistent safety challenges. The airport diagram, which you should have readily available during taxi operations, serves as your roadmap for understanding and following these instructions, and learning to visualize your position and route on it while simultaneously controlling the aircraft is another crucial skill. Yellow lines on the taxiway aren't decorative; they're essential navigation aids, with solid lines marking the centerline and dashed lines marking edges, while double solid yellow lines indicate hold-short positions beyond which you must never venture without explicit clearance.

Tower communications shift the focus skyward, focusing on the dynamic phases of takeoff, landing, and pattern work, where timing and sequence become critical. The simple phrase "cleared for takeoff" represents the only authorization that allows you to enter an active runway for departure; anything less, including "taxi into position and hold" or the newer phraseology "line up and wait," does not authorize takeoff itself. These distinctions matter enormously; pilots have attempted takeoffs with only position-and-hold clearances, sometimes with catastrophic results when another aircraft was already cleared to land on the same runway. When the tower clears you for takeoff, they're confirming that the runway is yours, there's no conflicting traffic, and you're authorized to begin your departure. Your acknowledgment should include your call sign: "Cleared for takeoff, runway three-six, Four-Five-Bravo," confirming both the instruction and the runway assignment. Landing clearances follow similar patterns, though tower controllers often add conditional clearances based on traffic: "Cherokee Four-Five-Bravo, number two following the Cessna on a two-mile final, runway three-six, cleared to land." You've been integrated into a sequence, given traffic to follow, and cleared for landing contingent on maintaining appropriate separation. If you can't see that Cessna, you need to speak up immediately: "Four-Five-Bravo has no visual on the traffic."

Tower will either help you locate the traffic or issue alternative instructions, but they can't manage separation if you falsely acknowledge traffic you haven't actually acquired. The pattern itself, that rectangular path in the sky around the airport, has its own terminology: upwind, crosswind, downwind, base, and final, each leg named for its relationship to the wind and the landing runway, and controllers use these terms to describe positions and issue instructions that pilots universally understand.

Departure and approach communications expose you to radar-based air traffic control. In this more complex environment, controllers monitor your target's movement on their screens and guide you through increasingly busy airspace. When departing a towered airport, the tower typically hands you off to departure control: "Cherokee Four-Five-Bravo, contact departure on one-two-four-point-six-five." This handoff requires you to check in with the new controller using a slightly different format: "Departure, Cherokee Two-Three-Four-Five-Bravo is with you, climbing through two thousand three hundred for four thousand five hundred." This initial call establishes your identity, confirms you're now on their frequency, and provides your current altitude and assigned altitude, giving the controller immediate situational awareness. Departure controllers see your aircraft as a radar target, complete with your altitude readout if you have an operating transponder, and they'll issue vectors —specific headings —to guide you clear of other traffic and on course toward your destination. The transponder, that mysterious box with four digits displayed, broadcasts a unique code that links your radar return to your flight information in the controller's computer. When they tell you to "squawk four-three-two-one," they're assigning you that specific code for identification. The emergency code seven-seven-zero-zero should be set immediately in any emergency, instantly alerting every controller who sees your target that you need priority handling, while seven-six-zero-zero indicates radio failure, and seven-five-zero-zero indicates a hijacking, codes so critical that pilots memorize them through the mnemonic "seven-five, man alive; seven-six, need a fix; seven-seven, going to heaven."

Uncontrolled airports introduce a different communication paradigm entirely, one based on self-announcing and cooperative separation rather than controller instructions. Without tower controllers to sequence traffic and issue clearances, pilots use a standard traffic advisory frequency — typically CTAF, the Common Traffic Advisory Frequency listed for each airport — to broadcast their positions and intentions to other aircraft in the area. These broadcasts follow a specific format designed to create a mental picture for other pilots: "Middleton traffic, Cherokee Four-Five-Bravo, left downwind, runway three-six, Middleton." The repeated use of the airport name at the beginning and end helps pilots distinguish between airports when monitoring multiple frequencies or when aircraft at different airports share the same CTAF, a common situation in some regions. Every significant position change warrants a broadcast: entering the pattern, turning base, turning final, and clearing the runway, creating a continuous stream of position reports that allow pilots to visualize where everyone is and anticipate potential conflicts. This system works remarkably well when everyone participates conscientiously, but it breaks down when pilots remain silent, make vague position reports, or incorrectly identify their location. The pilot who announces "taking the active" without specifying the runway or position, or, worse, takes off without any announcement at all, creates invisible danger that other pilots cannot anticipate or avoid. At uncontrolled fields, you're responsible for maintaining your own separation, visually acquiring other traffic, and sequencing yourself appropriately into the flow, challenges that require heightened awareness and excellent communication discipline. Some uncontrolled airports have remote communication outlets that allow you to access Flight Service for weather updates, or automated weather systems like AWOS or ASOS that broadcast current conditions, but these systems only provide information; they don't manage traffic or issue clearances.

Weather information threads through virtually every aviation communication, appearing in ATIS broadcasts, controller transmissions, pilot reports, and flight service briefings, all conveying critical information in standardized formats that compress maximum data into minimum time. The Automatic Terminal Information Service, ATIS, broadcasts a continuous loop of current airport conditions, assigned a phonetic letter that increments with each update. When you tell tower you have "information Delta," you're confirming you've received the specific weather observation, active runways, and operational notices contained in that broadcast, allowing the controller to skip reading you all that information individually. ATIS typically includes wind direction and velocity, visibility, cloud layers with their heights, temperature, dew point, altimeter setting, instrument approaches in use, landing runways, and any relevant notices, such as closed taxiways or construction. Learning to quickly extract and record this dense information stream while multitasking with other cockpit duties requires practice. Many students initially struggle with the rapid-fire delivery, missing critical details or confusing the numbers. Writing down the information systematically and developing your own shorthand notation for common elements helps ensure you capture everything essential. The altimeter setting, that seemingly simple number like "two-niner-niner-two," might be the single most critical piece of information you receive, as it allows your altimeter to display accurate altitude in the current pressure conditions, and setting the wrong altimeter can result in flying dangerously higher or lower than you believe. Pilot reports, PIREPs in aviation shorthand, add human observation to automated weather, with pilots describing actual conditions encountered aloft: "Moderate turbulence from six to nine thousand over the Millstone VOR, light rime icing in clouds." These reports directly influence other pilots' route and altitude decisions, creating a community of shared situational awareness.

Emergency communications carry unique urgency and protocol —procedures you hope never to use but must know thoroughly, because when they're needed, they're required immediately, with no time for reference or uncertainty. The simple word "Mayday" repeated three times declares an emergency requiring immediate priority handling, engine failure, fire, medical emergency, or any situation threatening the safety of the aircraft and its occupants. Saying "Mayday" instantly focuses every controller's attention on your situation and triggers a coordinated response to provide whatever assistance you need. If the problem is urgent but not immediately life-threatening — such as low fuel without yet declaring an emergency, or a rough-running engine that's still producing power — you preface your transmission with "Pan-pan" repeated three times, alerting controllers to your priority status without declaring a full emergency. The emergency broadcast follows a structured format when possible: who you're calling, your call sign, nature of the emergency, your intentions, your position, altitude, heading, number of persons on board, and fuel remaining. In reality, during an actual emergency, you communicate whatever information seems most relevant and trust that controllers will ask for anything else they need. The famous phrase "aviate, navigate, communicate" reminds pilots that flying the airplane and choosing a course of action take priority over talking on the radio; a crashed airplane with a perfect final transmission is still a crashed airplane. Controllers clear other traffic from your frequency, offer vectors to the nearest suitable airport, activate emergency services, and generally marshal resources to exemplify the aviation community's commitment to mutual support. Students practice emergency communications during training, making simulated distress calls that feel artificial but build the mental pathways needed for real emergencies when stress and workload threaten to overwhelm clear thinking.

Learning aviation radio communication represents a journey from painful self-consciousness through awkward competence to eventual fluency that rivals your native language in its automaticity. Early training flights involve students laboriously writing out their intended transmissions word-for-word, practicing them silently, then nervously keying the mic and reading the script in a quavering voice that broadcasts inexperience to everyone monitoring the frequency. Your instructor occupies the other seat, ready to intervene if you freeze or make a critical error, offering post-flight debriefs that dissect your communications with the same attention given to your aircraft control. Over time, you internalize the patterns, developing the ability to construct appropriate transmissions spontaneously without conscious effort, and to respond to controller instructions with the easy confidence that marks professional pilots. You learn to listen to other aircraft on frequency, building situational awareness about who's near you, what they're doing, and how the overall traffic flow is developing. You develop the ability to predict what controllers will likely say next based on the situation, positioning your hand near the frequency selector in anticipation of an imminent handoff or preparing your pen to copy an amended clearance. Your ear attunes to the subtle cues in controller voices, the slightly sharper tone when issuing a critical altitude restriction, the relaxed cadence when traffic is light and they have time for non-essential communication, the clipped urgency when the sector is saturated and every word must be essential. Eventually, you reach a level where communication becomes nearly unconscious, integrated seamlessly with your other flying skills, requiring no more focused attention than speaking to a passenger in everyday conversation. This fluency liberates mental resources for higher-level decision-making, situational awareness, and the pleasure of flying itself rather than the mechanics of talking about flying.

The standardization of aviation communication creates a universal language that transcends national boundaries, native languages, and cultural differences, enabling a pilot from any country to communicate effectively with controllers worldwide. English serves as aviation's international language, though the English spoken in aviation communications is really its own dialect. A limited vocabulary, standardized phrases, and the elimination of ambiguities make it learnable by pilots whose native languages range from Chinese to Spanish to Arabic. This universality ensures that whether you're flying into a small airport in rural Kansas or a central international hub in Southeast Asia, the fundamental communication patterns remain consistent and comprehensible. Regional variations certainly exist; American controllers tend toward more conversational tones while European controllers often sound more formal, and local idioms occasionally creep into transmissions, but the core structure remains standard. The International Civil Aviation Organization's Standards and Recommended Practices have created this harmonization through decades of work, continuously refining procedures based on safety data and operational experience. Learning this language well enough to participate effectively represents one of private pilot training's significant intellectual challenges, perhaps underestimated by those who assume flying is purely a physical skill. The mental agility required to simultaneously control an aircraft in three-dimensional space, navigate accurately, monitor systems, watch for traffic, and maintain professional radio communications while planning for what comes next demonstrates the complexity of even "simple" private pilot operations.

As you progress through training, you'll notice your relationship with radio communications fundamentally transforming. What initially seemed impossibly fast and confusing gradually becomes transparent and manageable. The calls that once required intense concentration to understand now register almost subconsciously, your brain extracting essential information while your conscious attention focuses elsewhere. You build confidence by requesting clarification when you miss a transmission, rather than pretending you understood and hoping for the best —a dangerous habit that's killed pilots who were too embarrassed to admit confusion. You learn when to speak and when to listen, developing the patience to wait for a gap in busy frequency chatter rather than stepping on other transmissions. You discover the subtle art of inflection and timing, how a well-placed pause can emphasize critical information, and how speaking just slightly slower than normal ensures clarity without sounding condescending. Most significantly, you realize that controllers aren't adversaries waiting to criticize mistakes, but professionals dedicated to keeping you safe, often remarkably patient with student pilots who identify themselves as such and ask questions when confused. The frequencies that once seemed exclusive and intimidating reveal themselves as what they truly are: essential tools for coordination, safety nets that keep thousands of aircraft operating in shared space without conflict, and the invisible infrastructure that makes modern aviation possible. Your growing proficiency in aviation communication marks your transition from outsider to participant, from observer to active member of the aviation community. This transformation ultimately matters as much as your ability to perform smooth landings or execute perfect steep turns.

Chapter 3: Ground School: Laying the Foundation

The sterile fluorescence of the classroom feels worlds away from the flight line, yet the transformation from aviation dreamer to licensed pilot truly crystallizes within these four walls. Ground school represents the intellectual scaffolding upon which all flight training rests, the place where abstract principles become concrete understanding, where the physics of flight transitions from mysterious force to predictable science. Many student pilots arrive at their first ground school session expecting dry lectures and tedious memorization, perhaps recalling uninspiring academic experiences from their past. What they discover instead is something far more captivating: a systematic unveiling of aviation's interconnected systems, each topic building upon the last, each concept revealing why aircraft behave as they do and how pilots harness natural laws to navigate three-dimensional space. The classroom becomes a laboratory of imagination where students visualize airflow over wings, trace weather patterns across continents, and decode the regulatory framework that keeps thousands of aircraft safely separated in shared airspace. Unlike previous educational experiences that might have felt disconnected from practical application, every ground school concept ties directly to situations students will encounter aloft, creating an urgency and relevance that transforms learning from obligation into opportunity.

The curriculum structure varies among flight schools: some offer intensive weekend seminars, others provide weekly evening sessions spread over several months, and still others offer self-paced online courses supplemented by periodic instructor check-ins. Regardless of format, the core content remains remarkably consistent, governed by Federal Aviation Administration requirements that establish minimum knowledge areas every private pilot must master. These topics span an impressive breadth, from the mechanical systems that keep engines running to the psychological factors that influence decision-making under pressure. A well-designed ground school program doesn't simply present these subjects as disconnected islands of information but weaves them together, demonstrating how weather knowledge informs flight planning, how aircraft systems understanding enables better emergency response, how aerodynamic principles explain performance limitations, and how regulations exist not as arbitrary restrictions but as lessons learned from decades of aviation experience. Students quickly realize they're not merely memorizing facts for an exam but instead constructing a comprehensive mental framework that will support every flight decision throughout their entire aviation career.

Aerodynamics forms the intellectual cornerstone of ground school, the fundamental science explaining how metal machines weighing thousands of pounds achieve and maintain flight. Beyond the elemental four forces already understood from earlier exposure to aviation concepts, ground school delves deep into the nuanced interactions between air and aircraft surfaces. Students explore how wing shape affects lift generation, discovering that the curved upper surface creates longer airflow paths compared to the flatter lower surface, resulting in pressure differentials that produce upward force. This deeper understanding extends to examining how the angle of attack —the angle between the wing's chord line and the oncoming airflow —critically determines lift production, with performance improving as the angle increases until the critical angle, where airflow separation occurs and the wing stalls. The beauty of comprehensive aerodynamics instruction lies in its practical applications: understanding why aircraft require longer takeoff distances on hot days, why turning flight demands increased back pressure to maintain altitude, why ice accumulation proves so dangerous, and why certain aircraft configurations produce specific handling characteristics. Instructors bring these concepts to life through demonstrations, using models to show airflow patterns, presenting video footage of flow visualization experiments, and, most powerfully, connecting classroom theory to students' actual flight experiences, asking them to recall sensations and observations from their recent lessons and explaining the aerodynamic phenomena underlying those experiences.

Aircraft systems knowledge transforms students from passive passengers into informed operators capable of managing complex machinery and responding effectively when systems malfunction. The typical training aircraft, though seemingly simple compared to commercial jets, contains remarkably sophisticated systems that demand a thorough understanding. The engine receives particular attention, with ground school exploring the four-stroke combustion cycle that converts fuel into mechanical power, the ignition system that provides redundant spark sources for safety, the fuel system that delivers precisely metered gasoline to cylinders, and the lubrication system that prevents destructive friction. Students learn to interpret engine instruments, understanding that oil temperature readings reveal internal health, that manifold pressure indicates engine power output, and that cylinder head temperature reflects combustion efficiency. The electrical system receives similar scrutiny, with instructions covering how the alternator generates power, how the battery provides backup capability, and how circuit breakers protect against electrical fires. Perhaps most crucially, ground school teaches systematic troubleshooting approaches, encouraging students to think methodically about system interdependencies rather than panicking when warning lights illuminate or gauges show unusual readings. This knowledge provides immense confidence, the understanding that most system issues present manageable challenges rather than immediate emergencies, and that proper diagnosis precedes effective response.

Weather theory constitutes perhaps the most intellectually demanding component of ground school, requiring students to grasp atmospheric physics, thermodynamics, and fluid dynamics while developing practical skills in forecast interpretation and risk assessment. The atmosphere reveals itself as a dynamic, constantly shifting environment where temperature variations drive air movement, moisture content determines cloud formation, pressure gradients create wind, and the interaction of air masses produces everything from gentle breezes to violent thunderstorms. Students explore the Standard Atmosphere model, learning how temperature and pressure decrease predictably with altitude under normal conditions, then discovering how real-world deviations from this model affect aircraft performance and weather development. Frontal systems are extensively examined, with instructions detailing how cold fronts produce rapidly moving boundaries with narrow bands of intense weather. In contrast, warm fronts create broader areas of gradually deteriorating conditions. The most engaging ground school instructors transform weather from abstract theory into vivid reality, presenting case studies of actual weather-related accidents, displaying time-lapse satellite imagery showing storm development, and teaching students to visualize three-dimensional atmospheric structures rather than viewing weather as merely what appears outside their window. Understanding concepts such as atmospheric stability, lifting mechanisms, and moisture processes enables students to examine morning skies and forecast afternoon developments, to read aviation weather products with genuine comprehension rather than superficial recognition, and to make sound cancellation decisions despite pressure to complete planned flights.

Regulations and airspace structure initially appear as aviation's most tedious subject, seemingly nothing more than memorization of arbitrary rules and boundaries. Yet proper instruction reveals this framework as carefully designed to manage complex operations while safely accommodating diverse user needs. The Federal Aviation Regulations governing private pilot operations fill hundreds of pages. Still, ground school focuses on the most operationally relevant provisions: pilot certification requirements, aircraft airworthiness standards, flight rules and operational limitations, and maintenance requirements. Students discover that most regulations stem from accident investigations, each rule representing a lesson learned —often tragically —by previous mistakes. The airspace system reveals similar logic, with Class A through G designations creating increasingly controlled environments based on traffic density and operational complexity. Understanding why Class B airspace surrounds major airports with strict entry requirements, why Class E begins at different altitudes in different locations, and why some areas remain uncontrolled Class G airspace transforms seemingly random classifications into a rational structure. Ground school instructors enhance regulatory instruction by emphasizing practical application rather than rote memorization, presenting scenarios requiring students to determine applicable regulations, providing memory aids that distill complex rules into memorable formats, and repeatedly reinforcing that regulations exist not to limit pilot freedom but to prevent the chaos that would inevitably result from uncoordinated operations.

Navigation training bridges ancient wayfinding principles with modern technology, teaching students multiple methods for determining position and planning routes while understanding each approach's strengths and limitations. Pilotage, the oldest navigation technique, relies on visual reference to landmarks and terrain features, requiring map-reading skills and environmental awareness. Dead reckoning builds a mathematical framework for navigation, using compass headings, airspeed measurements, and time calculations to predict positions and track progress. Ground school demystifies the mathematics underlying navigation, showing students how wind correction angles compensate for crosswinds, how true versus magnetic headings account for Earth's magnetic variations, and how to calculate fuel requirements with appropriate reserves. The real revelation comes when students discover that, despite their technological advances, sophisticated GPS systems fundamentally automate these traditional calculations rather than employ entirely different principles. Instructors emphasize that electronic navigation should enhance rather than replace foundational skills, sharing cautionary tales of pilots who became dangerously lost when their primary GPS failed because they had never developed backup capabilities. Chart reading receives substantial attention, with students learning to extract critical information from sectional aeronautical charts: terrain elevations, obstruction locations, airspace boundaries, airport frequencies, and countless other details compressed into dense graphical representations. The ability to glance at a chart and immediately grasp the operational environment separates proficient pilots from those who struggle with situational awareness.

Performance calculations and weight-and-balance computations transform flying from guesswork into precision engineering, providing mathematical tools that predict aircraft capabilities under specific conditions. Every aircraft operates within carefully defined limitations established by manufacturers through extensive testing, with performance varying dramatically based on weight, temperature, altitude, and configuration. Ground school teaches students to use performance charts and graphs, initially bewildering collections of lines and numbers that gradually resolve into powerful predictive tools. A student learns that their aircraft, fully loaded on a 95-degree day at a high-altitude airport, requires substantially more runway than the same aircraft, lightly packed, on a cool morning at sea level. These aren't merely academic exercises but potentially life-saving calculations, as exceeding performance limitations has caused countless accidents when pilots attempted operations their aircraft couldn't safely complete. Weight and balance calculations are equally critical, ensuring that aircraft remain within approved center-of-gravity ranges and exhibit predictable handling qualities. Loading an aircraft improperly, even within maximum weight limits, can create dangerous control difficulties or even render the aircraft uncontrollable. Ground school instruction typically progresses from simple weight-and-balance problems using standardized forms to more complex scenarios involving fuel burn adjustments and moment calculations, building competence through progressive practice until students can efficiently complete these essential preflight tasks.

Human factors and aeronautical decision-making represent relatively recent additions to ground school curricula, reflecting aviation's evolving understanding that technical proficiency alone doesn't ensure safety. Modern training emphasizes that pilots must recognize their own physical and psychological limitations and understand how fatigue, stress, illness, medication, alcohol, and altitude affect performance. The IMSAFE checklist, evaluating Illness, Medication, Stress, Alcohol, Fatigue, and Eating, provides a systematic personal assessment tool. Yet, ground school instruction extends far beyond acronyms to explore the subtle ways impairment manifests. Students learn that fatigue degrades judgment before affecting motor skills, that stress narrows attentional focus and increases error rates, that mild hypoxia produces euphoria that masks its own danger, and that humans consistently overestimate their capabilities while underestimating risks. Aeronautical decision-making models like DECIDE (Detect, Estimate, Choose, Identify, Do, Evaluate) structure the problem-solving process, providing frameworks that counter the natural human tendency toward impulsive reactions during stressful situations. Case studies are particularly valuable in this instruction, presenting actual scenarios in which pilot decision-making determined outcomes, asking students to identify decision points, evaluate available options, and consider how choices might have changed the results. These discussions reveal that most aviation accidents result not from single catastrophic failures but from chains of small decisions, each seemingly minor but collectively leading toward disaster, and that breaking these chains at any point through sound decision-making typically prevents tragedy.

Flight planning synthesizes nearly every ground school topic into a comprehensive preflight process that professional pilots execute before every flight. A thorough flight plan begins with defining the mission's purpose and constraints, then progresses through route selection, weather evaluation, aircraft performance assessment, fuel requirements calculation, alternate airport identification, and regulatory compliance verification. Ground school provides students with systematic planning procedures, typically starting with simplified scenarios on perfect-weather days, then progressively introducing complications: marginal weather requiring careful analysis, long distances requiring fuel stops, mountain terrain requiring performance calculations, and special-use airspace requiring coordination. Students discover that effective planning isn't merely filling out forms but rather thinking critically about every flight aspect, asking "what if" questions, and developing contingency options. What if forecast winds prove more potent than expected? What if the destination airport closes unexpectedly? What if the weather deteriorates en route? Having considered these scenarios during relaxed ground planning provides enormous advantages over attempting to develop solutions while managing aircraft control, navigation, and communication tasks simultaneously in flight. Modern flight planning increasingly incorporates electronic tools and applications that automate calculations and provide integrated weather briefings. Yet, ground school emphasizes understanding the underlying principles rather than unquestioningly trusting technology-generated outputs, teaching students to verify that computer-generated plans make operational sense.

Medical certification requirements and physiological factors affecting pilots receive thorough ground school coverage, as physical fitness directly impacts flight safety. Student pilots must obtain at least a third-class medical certificate from an FAA-designated Aviation Medical Examiner, verifying adequate vision, hearing, cardiovascular health, and neurological function. Ground school prepares students for this examination by explaining the standards and discussing common disqualifying conditions, while emphasizing that many medical issues can be addressed through special issuance processes. Beyond basic certification, instruction explores how the flight environment physiologically stresses human bodies in ways passengers rarely notice but pilots must manage. Hypoxia, oxygen deficiency at altitude, receives particular emphasis given its insidious nature and potentially rapid onset above 10,000 feet. Students learn to recognize early symptoms — increased breathing rate, lightheadedness, tingling sensations, and impaired judgment — and to understand why supplemental oxygen becomes legally required and physiologically essential at higher altitudes. Spatial disorientation, in which sensory conflicts produce false perceptions of aircraft attitude, underscores why instrument flying skills are crucial even for visual pilots, as inner-ear balance mechanisms can provide misleading information during flight maneuvers. Dehydration, carbon monoxide exposure, and vision limitations under different lighting conditions round out physiological instruction, with the overarching message that pilots must actively monitor their physical state rather than assuming they'll notice when capabilities degrade.

The ground school experience culminates in comprehensive examinations testing knowledge across all subject areas, first through the FAA written test and later through oral examination components of the practical test. The written exam, officially known as the Private Pilot Knowledge Test, contains 60 multiple-choice questions drawn from a large pool of possible items and requires students to demonstrate understanding of regulations, weather theory, navigation principles, aircraft systems, and aeronautical decision-making. Achieving the minimum passing score of 70 percent proves relatively straightforward for students who attended ground school attentively and completed practice tests, yet truly proficient pilots target scores in the 90-plus range, recognizing that knowledge gaps revealed by missed questions represent potential safety vulnerabilities requiring additional study. Many students focus excessively on passing this written exam, viewing it as the endpoint of ground school, yet experienced instructors emphasize that knowledge testing represents a beginning rather than an end, verifying baseline competency upon which all subsequent learning builds. The real validation arrives during the practical test's oral examination, when designated examiners probe understanding through scenario-based questions that require synthesizing multiple knowledge areas, explaining reasoning processes, and demonstrating judgment appropriate for a private pilot. These discussions can range widely, perhaps starting with flight planning for a cross-country trip, then diving into expected weather systems, examining how those conditions affect aircraft performance, exploring which regulatory requirements apply, and considering how student-pilot limitations factor into decision-making. Successfully navigating these comprehensive evaluations requires the deep, interconnected understanding that quality ground school instruction produces.

Beyond formal testing, ground school's most significant value manifests in how thoroughly educated pilots approach every aspect of aviation. A pilot who truly understands weather theory doesn't merely mechanically check forecasts; they visualize atmospheric conditions, recognize developing patterns, and make conservative decisions in marginal situations. A pilot who understands aircraft systems doesn't panic when unusual indications appear; instead, they methodically diagnose problems and execute appropriate responses. A pilot who has internalized regulatory frameworks operates confidently within the aviation system, understanding not only what the rules require but also why those requirements exist. This depth of knowledge transforms student pilots into aviators who think critically, question assumptions, and continuously seek to expand understanding rather than merely checking boxes on training requirements. The classroom discussions, the wrestling with complex concepts, the moments of sudden clarity when disparate topics connect —these experiences create lasting impressions that shape a pilot's mindset far more profoundly than any single fact memorized for an exam. Aviation instructors frequently observe that students who engaged deeply with ground school, who asked probing questions and sought genuine understanding, develop into safer, more competent pilots than those who viewed ground training as merely an obstacle to overcome before reaching the "real" training in the aircraft.

The integration of ground and flight training creates powerful learning synergies, with each domain reinforcing and illuminating the other. Concepts that seem abstract in the classroom become viscerally real during flight. At the same time, experiences that feel mysterious in the aircraft make perfect sense when examined through the analytical lens of ground school. A student who has studied aerodynamic theory in ground school recognizes slow-flight buffeting as the onset of airflow separation, understands why the instructor emphasizes specific recovery techniques, and can explain the physics underlying what they feel through the controls. Similarly, a student who has experienced turbulence during an afternoon flight session brings specific, tangible questions to ground school's weather instruction, seeking to understand the thermal activity that produced those bumps. Progressive flight schools deliberately coordinate ground and flight curricula, ensuring that classroom instruction precedes related flight lessons and that students receive conceptual frameworks before encountering phenomena firsthand. This sequencing prevents cognitive overload by allowing students to focus on skill development while recognizing and applying previously studied principles, rather than simultaneously managing aircraft control and processing entirely new concepts. Some schools even conduct ground instruction directly at airports, periodically moving from classroom to flight line to examine actual aircraft systems, observe weather conditions, and watch other aircraft operations, creating immediate connections between theory and practice.

The community aspect of ground school provides unexpected benefits, as students share perspectives, discuss challenges, and learn from each other's questions and insights. Unlike individual flight training, where students work one-on-one with instructors, ground school brings together diverse individuals united by common aviation aspirations. This group dynamic produces richer discussions than any single student-instructor interaction might generate, as different backgrounds and experience levels contribute unique viewpoints. A student with engineering training might offer mathematical explanations that help others grasp performance calculations, while someone with weather forecasting experience can supplement official instruction with practical observation techniques. Ground school classmates often form lasting friendships, continuing to share knowledge and support each other long after earning their certificates, creating informal networks that sustain aviation enthusiasm through the inevitable challenges every pilot faces. The questions one student raises frequently illuminate confusion others felt but hesitated to voice, creating permission for inquiry that enhances everyone's learning. Effective ground school instructors cultivate these supportive environments, encouraging questions, facilitating peer discussion, and ensuring that all students feel comfortable admitting uncertainty, recognizing that pretended understanding poses far greater dangers than acknowledged confusion.

As students progress through the ground school's comprehensive curriculum, a transformation occurs that extends beyond accumulated knowledge. They begin thinking like pilots, developing mental models that automatically consider multiple factors when evaluating situations, anticipate consequences before taking actions, and recognize risks that non-aviators never notice. This cognitive development represents ground school's ultimate achievement, the cultivation of an aeronautical mindset that characterizes professional aviators regardless of experience level. Standing outside watching aircraft operations, ground school graduates don't simply see planes taking off and landing; they analyze wind conditions based on traffic patterns, estimate density altitude effects from temperature and pressure, consider which weather factors might influence operations, and evaluate whether pilots are making sound decisions. This analytical perspective becomes automatic—an integral part of how trained pilots perceive the aviation environment—providing continuous learning opportunities throughout their flying careers as they observe, question, and refine their understanding with every airport visit and every flight. The classroom foundation laid during initial ground school supports this lifetime of learning, providing the fundamental framework upon which all subsequent knowledge builds. This solid footing allows pilots to climb ever higher in their understanding of aviation's infinite complexity and endless fascination.

The relationship between ground school instruction and long-term pilot competency is most evident during recurrent training and flight reviews, when pilots return years after initial certification to refresh their knowledge and skills. Aviation Safety Counselors and flight review instructors consistently report that pilots who developed a strong foundational understanding during ground school maintain proficiency far more effectively than those who merely memorized answers for the written test. The difference manifests in how pilots approach unfamiliar situations: those with solid theoretical grounding analyze new scenarios using fundamental principles, applying their understanding of aerodynamics, weather, and systems to reason through appropriate responses. In contrast, pilots lacking this foundation struggle when faced with conditions outside their narrow experience base, having never developed the analytical tools necessary to extrapolate from known situations to novel challenges. This distinction becomes particularly evident when regulations change or new technologies emerge, as aviation constantly evolves. Pilots with a deep understanding adapt readily, recognizing how new rules fit within existing frameworks or how modern equipment accomplishes traditional functions through different methods. Those who learned purely by rote find themselves perpetually struggling to keep current, unable to integrate new information because they never built the conceptual structures that enable integration.

The economic dimension of thorough ground school preparation deserves consideration, as comprehensive classroom education significantly reduces overall training costs despite requiring upfront investment. Students arriving at flight lessons with solid theoretical knowledge progress more efficiently through the practical curriculum, requiring fewer instructional hours to achieve proficiency because they're not simultaneously learning concepts and developing skills. They understand what instructors mean when discussing ground effect, adverse yaw, or load factor, allowing lessons to focus on recognizing and managing these phenomena rather than explaining basic principles. This efficiency translates directly into reduced flight time requirements and lower total training expenses. Additionally, well-prepared students pass written and practical examinations more reliably on their first attempts, avoiding the substantial costs of retesting. Perhaps most significantly, pilots who complete thorough ground school make better decisions throughout their aviation careers, avoiding the expensive mistakes, damaged aircraft, regulatory violations, and insurance claims that result from an inadequate understanding.

Flight school operators recognize these patterns, with many noting that their most successful students — those who complete training efficiently and become safe pilots — inevitably participate actively in ground school rather than treating it as a mere formality to endure.

Chapter 4: Into the Cockpit: First Solo Flight

The training area becomes familiar territory after weeks of dual instruction, its checkpoints and landmarks etched into memory like an aerial map inscribed directly onto consciousness. You recognize the distinctive bend in the river, the water tower on the hill, the intersection of highways that forms a perfect cross when viewed from three thousand feet. Yet on this particular morning, everything feels different. Your instructor completes the pre-flight briefing with words you've been simultaneously anticipating and dreading: today might be the day you fly alone. The statement hangs in the air between you, weighted with significance that transcends simple vocabulary. This represents the culmination of everything learned thus far —the moment when theory and practice converge into a single test of readiness. Your instructor has been watching, evaluating not just your technical proficiency but something more subtle and essential, your judgment, your decision-making under pressure, your ability to recover from mistakes without guidance. The endorsement to solo represents their professional assessment that you possess not merely adequate skills but the maturity and situational awareness necessary to operate an aircraft without supervision. This confidence must now transfer from instructor to student, a psychological handoff as crucial as any physical control of the plane.

The morning begins like countless others before it, with the familiar ritual of aircraft inspection. Your hands move across the aluminum skin with practiced efficiency, checking fuel sumps, testing control surfaces, examining tire wear, and propeller blades for damage. But awareness heightens today, sharpened by possibility. Every item on the checklist receives extra scrutiny, not out of distrust in previous inspections, but because you now bear sole responsibility. The concept of pilot-in-command has been discussed extensively during ground school and examined through case studies and regulatory frameworks, but understanding authority differs profoundly from exercising it. When your instructor occupies the right seat, ultimate accountability remains theirs —a safety net that allows learning through controlled mistakes. Remove that safety net, and decision-making acquires immediate, tangible consequences. The fuel gauges indicating full tanks, the engine oil level within acceptable limits, and the freedom from mechanical discrepancies; these routine confirmations suddenly feel like critical elements in a much larger equation. You sign the aircraft logbook with particular care, your signature affirming that this machine meets airworthiness standards, knowing that within hours, that same signature might precede your first solo endorsement.

The first flight of the day proceeds according to standard training patterns. Your instructor occupies the right seat, clipboard in hand, evaluating performance with the accumulated expertise of thousands of flight hours. Touch-and-goes fill the pattern work: landing, applying power, retracting flaps, and departing without ever coming to a complete stop. Each circuit around the pattern offers another opportunity to refine technique and to feel how the aircraft responds to control inputs during the critical phases of flight closest to the earth. Your approaches today demonstrate consistency, the airspeed settling into the narrow range that indicates proper descent management, and the touchdown point occurring within the designated zone marked on the runway. These technical achievements matter, certainly, but your instructor watches for something beyond mere numbers and procedures. They observe how you scan for traffic, your willingness to go around when an approach deteriorates, and your radio communications that balance brevity with necessary information. After the fifth landing, your instructor keys the intercom and suggests returning to the ramp. The words carry no particular emphasis, no hint of what follows, yet something in the delivery makes your pulse quicken.

Taxiing back to the parking area, your instructor breaks the silence with the question every student pilot both desires and fears: "Do you feel ready to take it around yourself?" The inquiry seems simple, almost casual, but embedded within those nine words lies profound significance. Your instructor isn't asking whether you believe you've memorized procedures or whether you think you can physically manipulate controls. They're asking whether you've achieved that elusive quality, confidence grounded in competence, that distinguishes someone prepared to solo from someone merely going through training motions. The question demands honest self-assessment, not bravado. Flight training attracts personalities comfortable with challenge, individuals willing to push boundaries, but safety requires acknowledging limitations. Saying yes means declaring yourself ready for one of aviation's defining moments. Saying no requires humility to recognize that readiness hasn't yet arrived, that additional dual instruction would better serve long-term goals than premature solo attempts driven by schedule or ego. Your answer emerges after a moment's consideration, delivered with conviction earned through preparation: yes, you're ready. Your instructor nods, expression neutral but eyes reflecting something that might be satisfaction, perhaps even pride in a student's progression.

The process of preparing for solo flight follows specific regulatory requirements and practical necessities. Your instructor exits the aircraft, but not before conducting final checks that extend beyond mechanical considerations. They review weather conditions one final time, confirming that winds remain within acceptable limits for your experience level, that visibility exceeds minimums, and that no thunderstorms lurk beyond the horizon. They verify that you carry appropriate documentation, including your student pilot certificate and your current, valid medical certificate. They remind you of radio frequencies, emergency procedures, and the exact pattern of flight expected: three takeoffs and landings, full stop each time, before taxiing back to the parking area. These instructions might seem redundant given weeks of training, but repetition serves a purpose. Under stress, complex information sometimes becomes inaccessible, but material reviewed immediately before critical events tends to remain available. Your instructor also removes their headset, kneeboard, and flight bag, small details that nevertheless create a noticeable difference. The right seat sits empty, an absence that feels more pronounced than mere physical vacancy. Some instructors place their headsets on the vacant seat, a symbolic presence and reminder that training hasn't concluded; it's merely entered a new phase. Others prefer a complete absence, forcing students to own the moment entirely.

Weight and balance calculations suddenly shift from academic exercise to practical reality as you prepare to taxi. The aircraft, without your instructor's weight, sits noticeably lighter and responds to control inputs in new ways. This change affects performance throughout the flight envelope, from acceleration during takeoff roll to climb rate to approach characteristics. During training, your instructor discussed these variations intellectually, perhaps demonstrated them during earlier flights, but experiencing them while alone adds a dimension that secondhand description cannot convey. The engine run-up proceeds according to the memorized checklist items, each switch and gauge confirming systems operate within normal parameters. Magneto checks show acceptable RPM drop, carburetor heat produces expected power reduction, and engine instruments display values within green arcs. But now, instead of glancing toward the right seat for a confirming nod, you make the determination yourself: the aircraft is ready, systems are nominal, conditions are suitable, and therefore flight can proceed. This independent verification represents more than a checkbox exercise; it exemplifies the judgment development that transforms students into pilots.

Taxiing toward the runway, radio communications take on heightened significance. The tower controller's voice, familiar from dozens of previous flights, sounds somehow different today, each instruction carrying weight that demands precise acknowledgment and compliance. You announce your position, request takeoff clearance, and receive the instruction you've heard countless times: "Cleared for takeoff runway two-seven, make left traffic." The words are identical to those spoken during previous flights, yet the meaning transforms when no instructor shares cockpit space. You acknowledge the clearance, taxi onto the runway centerline, and perform final checks: flight controls free and correct, trim set for takeoff, fuel selector on most of the tank, mixture rich. The mental checklist flows automatically, muscle memory developed through repetition, but consciousness remains heightened, aware that verification responsibility rests entirely with you. Before adding power, you scan the final approach path one last time, confirming that no aircraft are executing an emergency return and that no conflict exists that might invalidate your clearance despite tower authorization. This defensive awareness — looking beyond what controllers provide and maintaining a personal situational assessment — marks mature pilot thinking.

The takeoff roll begins with smooth, steady advancement of throttle to full power, and the aircraft responds with a familiar surge of acceleration. Airspeed indicator sweeps upward through forty knots, fifty, approaching rotation speed as white runway markers blur beneath the nose. At fifty-five knots, gentle back pressure on the yoke brings the nosewheel off pavement, and moments later, the main gear separates from earth. This sensation, experienced dozens of times with an instructor aboard, now carries a profound difference; you are flying alone. The ground falls away beneath you, the runway shrinking as altitude increases, and suddenly aviation's most fundamental truth crystallizes: you are pilot-in-command, solely responsible for this aircraft and its safe operation. The realization doesn't arrive as terror or panic but as acute awareness, consciousness sharpened to exceptional clarity. The engine produces steady power, the airspeed settles at seventy-five knots for the best rate of climb, and the altimeter winds clockwise through five hundred feet, eight hundred, approaching pattern altitude. Everything proceeds exactly as experienced during dual instruction, yet simultaneously feels entirely unprecedented. Some pilots describe this moment as exhilarating, others as sobering, but most acknowledge a quality difficult to articulate, the sensation of crossing a threshold that, once traversed, fundamentally alters one's relationship with aviation.

Leveling at pattern altitude requires the familiar sequence of power reduction, trim adjustment, and establishing cruise configuration, but without instructor oversight, each action demands deliberate attention. The habit of dividing responsibility — with the student handling controls while the instructor manages the radio or watches for traffic — no longer applies. You must simultaneously fly the aircraft, navigate the pattern, communicate with the tower, and maintain a vigilant scan for other traffic, integrating tasks that dual instruction allows to be distributed. This workload management represents crucial skill development, the ability to prioritize competing demands while ensuring no critical element receives inadequate attention. Turning crosswind, you glance at the empty right seat, its vacancy a persistent reminder of solitude aloft. Some students report talking to themselves during first solo flights, verbalizing checklist items and procedures as though the instructor still listens. Others maintain silence, internalizing the experience in ways that preclude description. Neither approach is correct nor incorrect; solo flight permits personal process without the need for explanation or justification. The aircraft responds to control inputs just as during dual instruction, obeying physical laws indifferent to pilot experience or certification status. Bank produces turn, pitch influences altitude, power controls airspeed; these relationships remain constant regardless of who occupies the cockpit.

Turning base leg, then final approach, the runway appears ahead, a rectangle of pavement that represents both destination and test. The approach must be managed with precision: airspeed within a narrow range, descent rate stable, power and pitch coordinated to intersect the proper glide path. Too high or too fast creates dangerous touchdown conditions; too low or too slow risks stall and loss of control. Your training has prepared you to make these adjustments —subtle throttle and yoke coordination that correct deviations before they become critical. Wind conditions require attention as well; crosswind components demand proper correction, headwinds and tailwinds affect the glide path and touchdown point. During dual instruction, your instructor offered verbal cues, suggestions, and corrections that supplemented your developing judgment. Now, that internal voice must suffice, assessing and adjusting based on accumulated experience and taught principles. The runway threshold passes beneath the nose; you reduce power to idle and execute the flare —the delicate transition from descent to level flight just above the runway that dissipates remaining energy and allows a gentle touchdown. The main wheels contact the pavement with a satisfying chirp, nosewheel settling moments later, and you've completed your first solo landing. The achievement registers intellectually before emotionally, with awareness that this landing, though similar to dozens practiced with an instructor aboard, carries entirely different significance.

The full-stop landing requires taxiing clear of the runway, backtaxiing to takeoff position, and preparing for the second departure. During this interval, emotions and thoughts may surface that have been suppressed —perhaps satisfaction, nervous energy now seeking release, or simply the acknowledgment of what you've accomplished and what remains. Two more patterns await completion before solo requirements are satisfied, but the most significant psychological hurdle has passed. You know now, with certainty born of experience rather than belief, that you can safely fly and land an aircraft alone. This knowledge builds confidence that propels remaining circuits. The second takeoff feels more natural and less novel as the brain integrates new experiences into existing frameworks. The pattern work proceeds with growing comfort, though vigilance never relaxes. Complacency represents a persistent danger in aviation —the subtle erosion of attention that occurs when tasks become routine. Your training emphasized this threat, citing statistics demonstrating that accidents cluster not only among inexperienced pilots but also during phases when familiarity breeds inattention. Each landing demands the same careful approach, the same precise speed management, regardless of whether it's your first or your thousandth.

The third and final pattern brings a mixture of relief and unexpected reluctance. Relief because the test nears completion, reluctance because this singular experience, the first solo flight, can never be repeated. Aviation offers many milestone moments throughout a pilot's career: first cross-country, first instrument approach in actual conditions, first flight in a new aircraft type. Each carries significance and satisfaction. But first, solo occupies a unique position —the moment when student status begins a genuine transformation toward pilot identity. The final approach mirrors the previous two, stabilized descent guided by familiar sight pictures and instrument references. The landing, if anything, feels smoother than earlier attempts, perhaps because accumulated comfort has relaxed excess muscle tension that sometimes degrades control touch. Wheels kiss pavement, you taxi clear, and key the radio to inform the tower that you're concluding training for the day. The controller's acknowledgment might include congratulations if they're aware you've just soloed, or a small recognition from the aviation community welcoming a new member. Taxiing back to parking, the aircraft feels simultaneously familiar and transformed, no longer merely a machine in which you've received instruction but a partner in achievement. This vessel carried you across a critical threshold.

Your instructor waits at the ramp, and their expression tells you everything before they speak. Pride shines through professional reserve, satisfaction in a student's success that represents teaching's deepest reward. The post-flight debrief reviews each pattern, discussing what went well and identifying areas for continued development. Even successful solo flights reveal opportunities for improvement: an approach that could have been more stabilized, a radio call that lacked clarity, a traffic scan that momentarily lapsed. These observations don't diminish accomplishment but contextualize it within the broader scope of ongoing development. Aviation learning never truly ends; even airline captains with decades of experience continue refining their techniques and expanding their knowledge. Your instructor's feedback serves this developmental purpose, celebrating achievement while maintaining the perspective that solo represents a milestone rather than a destination. They complete your logbook endorsement with particular care, their signature and instructor number certifying that you have met the requirements of Federal Aviation Regulations and demonstrated the competence necessary for solo flight. This endorsement holds legal and practical significance, authorizing specific operations within defined parameters. More importantly, it represents professional validation, your instructor's public statement that you have earned the trust to operate aircraft independently.

The tradition of shirttail cutting, though practiced less universally than in aviation's earlier decades, sometimes follows first solo flights. The custom originated when instructors sat behind students in tandem-seat aircraft, making verbal communication difficult. Upon successful solo, the instructor would cut away the student's shirttail and inscribe it with flight details, date, aircraft type, and airport, creating a tangible memento of achievement. Modern training typically occurs in side-by-side configurations with intercoms, rendering the original practical purpose obsolete, but some instructors maintain the tradition for ceremonial value. Whether or not shirttails are cut, some form of recognition usually marks the occasion. Photographs document the moment, capturing expressions that blend satisfaction, relief, and perhaps lingering adrenaline. These images later serve as reminders during challenging phases of training, evidence that you can overcome obstacles and achieve goals that require sustained effort. Fellow students, if present, offer congratulations that carry particular weight; they understand better than non-pilots the significance of what you've accomplished, having either achieved their own solos or working toward them.

Reflection often follows first solo flights, a mental processing that occurs over the subsequent hours and days as the experience integrates into broader self-conception. The flight itself typically lasts only twenty to thirty minutes — three brief circuits around a familiar pattern — but the impact resonates far beyond that narrow timeframe. You've demonstrated to yourself and others that you can safely operate complex machinery in three-dimensional space, making time-critical decisions with incomplete information while managing multiple simultaneous demands on attention. These skills transfer beyond aviation, developing confidence and competence that inform other life domains. The experience also reveals areas requiring continued development and honest self-assessment that distinguish effective learning from empty credential collection. Perhaps radio communications felt rushed, words tumbling out faster than necessary. Possibly airspeed control during approach varied more than ideal, requiring constant throttle adjustments. Possibly, traffic scanning lapsed during intense focus on landing execution. These observations inform subsequent training priorities, directing practice toward specific areas for improvement rather than generic repetition.

The practical implications of solo endorsement extend beyond emotional satisfaction or traditional recognition. This achievement unlocks training activities that were previously impossible during dual instruction phases. Solo practice allows the development of personal techniques and the building of confidence through repetition, without an instructor's presence influencing decision-making. The landing pattern work that consumed your first solo flight will be repeated many times, developing consistency and automaticity that transforms conscious effort into fluid execution. Emergency procedures receive solo practice as well, simulated engine failures, and forced landing approaches that test judgment without backup available. Cross-country flight planning, navigation, and execution ultimately occur solo as well, preparing for the long-distance flights required for private pilot certification. Each solo flight builds upon previous experience, gradually expanding operational boundaries while developing the judgment that keeps expansion safe. The endorsement carries limitations as well, restrictions that recognize solo students occupy an intermediate position between a complete novice and a certificated pilot. Weather minimums for solo flight exceed those for private pilots, requiring greater visibility and lower winds. Solo students cannot carry passengers, cannot fly for compensation, and must operate within geographical boundaries defined by their instructor. These limitations protect both the student and others, ensuring that expanded independence occurs within safety parameters appropriate for the experience level.

Looking forward, solo flight represents roughly the midpoint of private pilot training. Significant work remains before checkride day, when a designated pilot examiner will evaluate your knowledge and skills across all required areas. But the psychological transformation initiated by solo flight fundamentally alters remaining training. Confidence builds differently when you know from personal experience that you can handle the aircraft independently. Subsequent dual instruction shifts from basic control teaching toward refinement and expansion, introducing more complex scenarios and honing judgment for situations that demand nuanced response. The instructor evolves from a primary operator who occasionally allows you to fly into a consultant and evaluator who watches you operate while providing guidance. This change in relationship reflects your development from learning the fundamentals to developing a pilot and preparing for certification. The empty right seat during solo flights becomes less jarring with experience, eventually feeling natural rather than notable. You create internal dialogue —questioning and answering yourself, evaluating decisions, and adjusting techniques — without external input. This internal instructor voice, once developed, persists throughout an aviation career, providing self-monitoring that enhances safety even when flying alone decades later.

The path from first solo to private pilot certificate winds through additional requirements: cross-country flights to unfamiliar airports, night operations when ground features disappear and spatial orientation challenges multiply, hood work simulating instrument conditions, and a comprehensive review preparing for written and practical examinations. Each component builds upon foundations established during earlier training while adding new dimensions of complexity and capability. But none quite match the first solo's psychological significance, that moment when you discovered through direct experience that you possess what it takes to fly alone. Other pilots understand this truth through shared experience, a bond that transcends differences in aircraft type, mission, or career trajectory. Ask any pilot about their first solo, and you'll often see their expression shift, memory transporting them back to that specific day, that particular aircraft, those unforgettable moments aloft without instructor presence. The details vary — different airports, different aircraft, different weather — but the emotional core remains constant: pride in achievement, respect for aviation's demands, and recognition that you've joined a community defined by those willing to accept the responsibilities of flight. The empty right seat, initially unsettling, becomes a symbol of independence earned through dedication, proof that skyward dreams, when pursued with commitment and proper guidance, transform from aspiration into accomplished reality.

The days following the first solo often bring unexpected emotional complexity, reactions that surface once immediate intensity subsides. Some students report feeling invincible, with confidence soaring to levels that concern instructors, who recognize that overconfidence poses dangers equal to timidity. Others experience doubt, questioning whether their successful solo was due to skill or merely to fortunate conditions, and wondering whether they can replicate the performance consistently. Both responses represent standard psychological processing of significant achievement under stress. Your instructor, having guided many students through this transition, watches for these patterns, ready to provide perspective that contextualizes emotional extremes within a broader developmental arc. They understand that confidence must be calibrated —sufficient to support independent operation yet tempered by a realistic assessment of current limitations and the learning that remains.

The solo endorsement also shifts relationships with non-flying friends and family members, who may struggle to comprehend what you've accomplished. Describing the experience to those outside aviation often proves challenging, as the technical details mean little without context, while the emotional significance resists easy articulation. You've achieved something that most people will never attempt, operated machinery in an environment where mistakes carry immediate, potentially severe consequences, and demonstrated competence that professional instructors validated through their endorsement. Yet explaining this to someone who's never considered pilot training often results in polite congratulations that lack genuine understanding of the milestone's magnitude. Fellow pilots, conversely, require no explanation; mention your first solo, and recognition appears instantly in their expressions, accompanied by knowing nods and often their own remembered stories. This shared understanding creates connections across generations of aviators, a continuity of experience linking today's student pilots with those who soloed decades earlier in different aircraft but identical circumstances of solitary flight.

Weather awareness intensifies after solo endorsement, as you gain personal responsibility for go-no-go decisions that previously rested with instructors. Morning skies are scrutinized by casual observers, who note cloud heights, visibility, wind direction, and forecast trends to determine whether solo practice can proceed safely. This meteorological attention develops habits that serve throughout aviation careers, ingraining the discipline of conservative weather assessment that prevents accidents born from optimism overriding prudence.

Chapter 5: Navigating the Clouds: Mastering Maneuvers

The transition from fundamental aircraft control to precision maneuvering represents a pivotal evolution in pilot development, transforming mechanical stick-and-rudder skills into genuine airmanship. After achieving the milestone of solo flight, training intensifies toward mastering the specific maneuvers that demonstrate complete command of the aircraft across its operational envelope. These maneuvers —steep turns, slow flight, stalls, ground reference exercises, and emergency procedures —form the practical examination standards that every private pilot candidate must demonstrate to FAA examiners. Yet their significance extends far beyond checkride requirements. Each maneuver teaches fundamental principles about aerodynamics, aircraft limitations, spatial awareness, and energy management that pilots apply throughout their flying careers. The steep turn reveals the relationship between bank angle and loading forces. Slow flight exposes the margins between controlled flight and aerodynamic stalling. Power-off stalls demonstrate what happens when airflow across wings becomes insufficient to generate lift. These lessons, practiced repeatedly in the relative safety of training scenarios, build the muscle memory and intellectual understanding that prevent accidents when unexpected situations arise during real-world flying. Instructors structure this training phase methodically, introducing maneuvers sequentially by complexity and building on previously developed skills. Students discover that mastering these exercises requires synthesizing everything learned previously — aircraft control, situational awareness, radio communication, and weather assessment — into integrated performances that demand simultaneous attention to multiple variables. The cockpit becomes an orchestra, with pilots making continuous adjustments to power, pitch, bank, and trim while monitoring altitude, airspeed, heading, coordination, and external references. This orchestration distinguishes between adequate and exceptional pilots, revealing whether foundational skills have truly taken root or merely received superficial attention.

Steep turns introduce pilots to the profound effects of loading forces on aircraft performance, demonstrating that aviation physics operates differently from ground-based intuition. The maneuver requires entering a precisely coordinated turn at a forty-five-degree bank angle while maintaining constant altitude and airspeed throughout a complete three-hundred-sixty-degree revolution. What appears straightforward in concept becomes surprisingly challenging in execution because the increased bank angle fundamentally alters the aircraft's behavior. At 45° of bank, the wings generate lift in two directions simultaneously: vertically to counteract gravity and horizontally to turn the plane, resulting in a loading factor of approximately 1.4 Gs. This increased loading means the aircraft effectively weighs forty percent more than usual, requiring additional power and back pressure to maintain altitude. Wings must work harder to support this increased apparent weight, pushing the aircraft closer to stalling speed even while the airspeed indicator shows cruise velocity. First attempts at steep turns invariably result in altitude losses as pilots discover that standard power settings cannot sustain level flight under these conditions. The nose drops despite pulled-back control yokes, altitude bleeds away, and the aircraft begins descending in a tightening spiral. Instructors demonstrate proper technique: adding power as the bank increases, applying firm back pressure to lift the nose, using outside references to detect altitude changes before instruments confirm them, and trimming carefully to reduce control pressures. Students practice repeatedly, developing the anticipation necessary to make continuous micro-adjustments that keep altitude within the hundred-foot tolerance standards. The maneuver teaches energy management principles applicable throughout aviation: understanding that maneuvering costs energy through increased drag and induced lift requirements; recognizing when additional power is necessary; and appreciating how loading factors affect stall speeds and structural limits. Commercial pilots later use these same principles when maneuvering near terrain, and instrument pilots apply them when holding patterns require steep turns in weather. The steep turn serves as a laboratory for exploring aircraft performance boundaries in a controlled environment where mistakes produce learning rather than accidents.

Slow flight operations expose pilots to the edges of controllability, where aircraft responsiveness diminishes and unusual handling characteristics emerge. The exercise requires establishing and maintaining flight at a minimum controllable airspeed, typically 5 to 10 knots above stalling speed, while performing specific maneuvers such as climbs, descents, and turns. At these reduced velocities, airflow across control surfaces decreases dramatically, making the aircraft feel mushy and unresponsive compared to normal cruise speeds. Control inputs that produce immediate reactions at ninety knots generate delayed, sluggish responses at fifty knots. The aircraft wallows through the air, wings pitched at high angles of attack to create sufficient lift at reduced speed, requiring substantial back pressure on the yoke to maintain level flight. Students initially overcontrol, making significant inputs that produce exaggerated reactions after notable delays, leading to pilot-induced oscillations as they constantly chase changing flight parameters. The experience teaches patience and finesse, developing an understanding that aircraft respond differently across their speed range and that effective control requires adapting techniques to prevailing conditions. Instructors emphasize recognizing the sensory cues that indicate the approach to slow flight: reduced wind noise, altered engine sounds, a mushy control feel, an increased nose-high attitude, and pronounced airflow buffeting that vibrates through the airframe. These cues become critical during landing approaches, when pilots must recognize inadvertent speed reductions before they escalate into dangerous situations. Slow flight training also introduces configuration management, as students practice extending flaps to varying degrees to explore how these devices alter stalling speeds, control effectiveness, and descent rates. Transitioning between clean configurations and full flaps while maintaining constant altitude and heading requires careful power management and trim adjustments, teaching coordination skills applicable to every traffic pattern and approach. The maneuver builds awareness of energy states, helping pilots recognize when aircraft possess adequate performance margins versus situations where reserves have diminished dangerously. This awareness becomes critical during go-around decisions, when pilots must instantly assess whether remaining performance is sufficient for a safe climb or whether terrain and obstacles pose a collision threat.

Stall recognition and recovery training confronts pilots with the fundamental limitation that governs all conventional aircraft, the critical angle of attack beyond which wings cannot generate sufficient lift regardless of airspeed or power settings. Private pilot training requires demonstrating proficiency in power-off stalls simulating landing configurations, power-on stalls simulating departure scenarios, and accelerated stalls showing that excessive maneuvering can induce stalling at any airspeed. These exercises deliberately push aircraft to the aerodynamic breaking point, where smooth airflow separates from the wing surfaces, lift collapses abruptly, and controlled flight ceases unless pilots execute proper recovery techniques. The sensations during stall progression create discomfort initially: the deck angle rises steeply as pilots pull back more elevator, airspeed decays despite full power, the stall warning horn sounds insistently, buffeting vibrates through the control surfaces, and finally the aircraft pitches downward or drops a wing as lift disappears. Natural human instincts scream to pull back harder on the yoke to avoid the nose-down pitching sensation. Yet this instinct worsens the situation by increasing the angle of attack further. Proper recovery requires counterintuitive actions: pushing forward decisively to decrease the angle of attack below critical levels, simultaneously applying full power to arrest altitude loss, and coordinating rudder pressure to prevent secondary stalls during recovery. Instructors emphasize that altitude loss during recovery remains acceptable and expected; attempting to minimize it by pulling back prematurely restalls the aircraft and compounds the problem. Students practice these recoveries repeatedly until proper reactions become automatic, overriding instinctive responses with trained procedures that restore controlled flight efficiently. The training addresses common variations, including accelerated stalls that occur during steep turns when pilots pull excessive back pressure attempting to maintain altitude, demonstrating that stalling depends on angle of attack rather than airspeed alone. A clean aircraft stalls at fifty-eight knots in level flight, but might stall at seventy-five knots while maneuvering under high loading. This understanding proves critical during traffic patterns where pilots banking steeply from base to final while pulling back to arrest descent can inadvertently stall at approach speeds that typically provide adequate margins.

Ground reference maneuvers develop the three-dimensional spatial awareness necessary for operating safely in the airport environment and navigating accurately across terrain. These exercises, including rectangular courses, S-turns across roads, and turns around a point, require maintaining specific relationships with ground features while constantly adjusting for wind drift. Unlike flying at altitude, where wind affects groundspeed but not heading control, low-altitude maneuvering exposes pilots to the reality that wind continuously pushes the aircraft, requiring constant heading corrections to maintain desired ground tracks. The rectangular course simulates traffic pattern operations, flying a precise rectangle around a section of countryside while maintaining constant altitude and distance from boundaries despite changing wind corrections on each leg. When flying perpendicular to wind direction, drift pushes the aircraft toward or away from the reference line, requiring angled headings that appear incorrect relative to the desired ground track but compensate perfectly for wind effects. Turning at corners requires rolling into the bank early when turning from downwind to crosswind legs, because tailwind components increase groundspeed, causing the aircraft to overshoot the desired position unless pilots anticipate the effect. Conversely, turning from upwind to crosswind requires delayed roll-ins because slower groundspeeds mean the aircraft covers less distance during turns. Students initially struggle with these adjustments, either crabbing at awkward angles that feel wrong despite producing correct ground tracks or maintaining comfortable headings that result in terrible ground positions. The exercise trains pilots to trust what they observe externally rather than what feels correct internally, developing the external-reference orientation necessary for visual navigation. S-turns across roads add complexity by requiring continuous radius adjustments throughout each half-circle, beginning with steep banks immediately after crossing the road when downwind groundspeed is highest, then gradually shallowing the bank as the turn progresses and groundspeed decreases on crosswind and upwind segments. Turns around a point demand even greater finesse, maintaining a perfect circle around a ground reference while varying bank angle throughout the three-hundred-sixty-degree revolution to compensate for constantly changing wind correction requirements. These maneuvers teach wind-correction skills essential for landing, where pilots must continuously adjust their approach paths to maintain runway alignment despite crosswind components that push the aircraft laterally.

Emergency procedures training addresses the psychological dimensions of aviation safety, building the mental preparation needed to respond effectively when systems fail unexpectedly. Engine failures are practiced extensively through simulated scenarios in which instructors suddenly reduce throttle to idle at random moments during maneuvers, forcing students to transition immediately from normal operations to emergency protocols. The startle factor never entirely disappears, regardless of how many practice repetitions occur, because humans instinctively react with surprise when engines stop producing reassuring sounds of power. Training focuses on overcoming this startle response through memorized, immediate action items that become automatic: establishing the best glide airspeed to maximize available time and distance, identifying suitable landing areas within gliding range, and initiating turns toward the selected field while altitude permits maneuvering. Students learn that altitude represents the only resource available during power-off flight, a finite commodity that must be managed carefully through precise airspeed control and efficient maneuvering. Flying too slowly wastes altitude due to excessive drag, without extending range significantly, and flying too fast burns altitude quickly while covering the same distance achievable at proper glide speed. The training emphasizes accepting that off-airport landings will occur if no suitable runways lie within gliding distance, and that pilots can dramatically improve survival outcomes by controlling the aircraft all the way to touchdown rather than attempting desperate maneuvers that might regain airports at the cost of stalling or spinning into terrain. Instructors demonstrate the mental discipline required to complete checklists methodically during emergencies, rather than fixate on single solutions, teaching students to verify fuel selector positions, check magneto switches, confirm primer locks, and attempt restart procedures while simultaneously managing the flight path and preparing landing areas. Equipment failures beyond engine problems also receive attention, including electrical failures requiring continued operation on battery power until landing, vacuum pump failures that render gyroscopic instruments inoperative, and communication radio failures necessitating light-gun signals from control towers. These scenarios build resilience and adaptability, teaching pilots that successful outcomes depend on maintaining aircraft control regardless of equipment status rather than becoming overwhelmed by cascading complications.

Crosswind landing techniques challenge pilots to operate safely in conditions where wind flows across runways at angles rather than along the landing direction. Most aircraft can handle crosswind components of 15 to 20 knots successfully with proper techniques, but these operations require skills beyond straightforward calm-wind landings. The fundamental challenge is maintaining runway alignment while compensating for wind that tries to push the aircraft to the side during approach and touchdown. Two primary techniques exist, each with advantages in specific situations. The crab method maintains wings level while angling the fuselage into the wind, flying an approach path that appears misaligned with the runway until just before touchdown, when pilots kick rudder to straighten the nose while simultaneously lowering the upwind wing to prevent drift. The slip method establishes a cross-controlled state throughout the final approach, reducing the upwind wing's drift while applying opposite rudder to maintain runway alignment, creating a balanced condition in which the aircraft tracks straight down the centerline despite angled control inputs. Students initially find cross-controlled flight uncomfortable because it violates the coordination principles emphasized during basic training, creating a sensation of sliding sideways through the air while maintaining a straight ground track. The technique requires continuous adjustments as wind velocity and direction change throughout descent, demanding precise coordination between aileron and rudder inputs that maintain alignment while preventing drift. Touchdowns occur on the upwind central wheel first, then the downwind wheel contacts as the aircraft settles, and finally the nosewheel touches after adequate weight transfers to the main gear. This staged touchdown sequence prevents side-loading landing gear, which could cause structural damage or loss of directional control. Instructors emphasize recognizing personal limitations and aircraft capabilities, teaching students that specific crosswind components exceed safe operating parameters regardless of technique proficiency. These situations require diverting to alternate airports with more favorable runway orientations rather than attempting landings that push beyond prudent limits. The training builds judgment alongside skill, developing the self-awareness necessary for making conservative decisions that prioritize safety over completion pressures.

Precision landing exercises refine the touchdown accuracy necessary for operating into short fields or avoiding obstacles on approach paths. These maneuvers require planning descents that arrive at specific touchdown points rather than merely reaching runways somewhere within their available length. The training addresses scenarios in which excess airspeed cannot be burned off with extended floats because obstacles or insufficient runway length preclude the necessary margins. The short-field technique begins during downwind legs with early power reductions and gradual descents that establish final approach speeds just above stalling velocity — typically 50 to 60 knots, depending on aircraft type — while maintaining steeper-than-normal descent angles that clear obstacles at the runway threshold. Students learn to use specific flap configurations and power settings that produce stable, controllable descents without requiring excessive speed margins. The aircraft arrives at the runway threshold with obstacle clearance, then continues descending at controlled rates until the main wheels contact the pavement firmly at the designated touchdown point. Instructors emphasize avoiding the temptation to flare excessively, which wastes valuable runway distance during touchdown floats. Instead, pilots establish nose-high attitudes just sufficient to break the descent rate, then hold the positions until the wheels firmly contact the ground. After touchdown, maximum aerodynamic braking occurs through maintaining nosewheel elevation while applying heavy main-wheel braking until speed decreases enough that continued nosewheel elevation would risk tail strikes, then lowering the nose and continuing maximum braking until safe taxi speeds. Soft-field techniques address the opposite scenario, where runway surfaces might be muddy, snow-covered, or unpaved, creating conditions in which nosewheels could dig in and cause aircraft to flip forward or bog down if excessive weight is transferred forward. These procedures require maintaining nosewheel elevation throughout the takeoff roll and keeping weight off the nosewheels after landing by applying continuous back pressure until the aircraft is slow enough to require nosewheel lowering. The training builds pilot capabilities for operating in diverse environments beyond the comfortable confines of towered airports with seven-thousand-foot paved runways, expanding operational possibilities while developing the judgment needed to assess field conditions and determine whether safe operations remain feasible.

Night flying operations introduce sensory limitations that fundamentally alter how pilots perceive environments and operate aircraft. Visual references that remain obvious during daylight conditions become invisible or misleading after darkness eliminates terrain detail and reduces depth perception. Horizons blur into indistinct transitions between earth and sky, making attitude control challenging when outside references disappear. Students discover that instruments serve as primary attitude references even during visual flight conditions because natural horizons cannot be reliably distinguished. The training occurs in stages, beginning with local-area orientation flights at familiar practice sites to demonstrate how darkness transforms recognizable landmarks into confusing patterns of light that bear little resemblance to their daytime appearance. The distinctive river bend, visible from miles away during afternoon flights, disappears at night unless moonlight reflects off the water's surface. The water tower, which serves as a reliable checkpoint during daytime operations, blends into the surrounding terrain unless its lights are operational. Roads remain visible through vehicle headlights that trace paths across the countryside, though distinguishing between highways and local streets becomes difficult without familiarity. Urban areas create glowing pools of light pollution that obscure stars and make identifying specific cities challenging until pilots learn to recognize patterns of interstate highways or airport beacon arrangements. Traffic pattern operations at night demand different visual techniques because runway edges blend into the surrounding terrain unless marked by lighting systems. Pilots learn to judge altitude and descent rates through relationships between runway lights and aircraft position rather than through ground texture and height perception available during daylight conditions. The training emphasizes conservative approaches to night operations, avoiding unfamiliar airports without adequate lighting, maintaining higher altitude reserves during cross-country flights, planning routes over populated areas where emergency landing options remain available, and accepting that weather minimums require more conservative interpretation when darkness eliminates ceiling and visibility assessment capabilities. Night flying offers unique rewards, including smoother air due to temperature stabilization after sunset, reduced traffic congestion, and extraordinary visual experiences, such as watching city lights stretch to the horizon or seeing distant thunderstorms illuminate clouds from hundreds of miles away. Students emerge from night training with expanded capabilities and heightened respect for the limitations darkness imposes on visual flight operations.

Advanced airwork integrates previously learned maneuvers into complex scenarios that demand simultaneous management of multiple tasks while maintaining precise aircraft control. These exercises combine maneuvering with navigation, radio communication, weather assessment, and traffic avoidance, creating workload levels that approximate real-world cross-country flight conditions. Instructors assign scenarios requiring flights to unfamiliar practice areas, using pilotage and dead-reckoning navigation, while performing steep turns, slow flight, and stall series at designated checkpoints, then returning to airports through busy airspace, requiring radio coordination with approach controllers. Students discover that workload management becomes critical when multiple demands compete for attention at the same time. Attempting to complete maneuver checklists while watching for traffic, monitoring navigation progress, and communicating with controllers can overwhelm pilots who have not developed systematic scan patterns and task-prioritization skills. The training teaches strategies for distributing attention efficiently: completing aircraft configuration changes before beginning maneuvers rather than during them, using level-flight segments for reviewing procedures and updating navigation, requesting frequency changes during straight flight rather than while turning, and recognizing when workload exceeds capacity and refusing additional task assignments until existing responsibilities receive adequate attention. This honest self-assessment is critical to safety because pilots who accept tasks beyond their capabilities create dangerous situations in which aircraft control deteriorates while attention is focused elsewhere. Instructors emphasize the aviation axiom that maintaining aircraft control trumps all other responsibilities. If choosing between accurate navigation and maintaining altitude, altitude takes priority because navigation errors can be corrected easily, while altitude deviations may pose collision hazards. The integrated scenarios also introduce decision-making exercises in which the weather deteriorates, fuel levels drop below anticipated levels, or passengers become airsick, requiring pilots to assess situations and determine appropriate courses of action. These exercises build the aeronautical decision-making skills that separate pilots who complete flights safely from those who press beyond prudent limits and create accident statistics. Students learn to recognize hazardous attitudes, including anti-authority resistance to following procedures, impulsivity, making decisions without adequate consideration, invulnerability, assuming accidents happen to others, macho attempts to prove capabilities, and resignation, accepting outcomes as inevitable rather than taking action to improve situations. Recognizing these attitudes within themselves and applying antidotes becomes part of the mental discipline that professional aviation demands.

Checkride preparation crystallizes all previous training into polished performances that demonstrate mastery of practical test standards. The FAA establishes specific performance criteria that examiners use to evaluate pilot competency, including altitude maintenance tolerances of plus-or-minus 100 feet during maneuvers, heading control within 10 degrees, and airspeed management within 10 knots of target values. These standards represent minimum acceptable performance levels rather than indicators of excellence, yet achieving them consistently under examination pressure challenges even well-prepared students. Instructors conduct mock checkrides that simulate actual examination conditions, evaluate performance using the same standards FAA examiners will employ, and provide detailed feedback on deficiencies that require additional practice. Students discover that performing maneuvers flawlessly during regular training flights does not guarantee checkride success because examination pressure creates distractions that degrade performance. The knowledge that an examiner is evaluating every action, combined with awareness that failures require expensive repeat examinations and training delays, produces stress responses that interfere with smooth execution. Hands shake slightly during control inputs, scan patterns become erratic, and memory blocks occur when attempting to recite checklist items. The mock checkride process desensitizes students to examination pressures through repeated exposure, transforming extraordinary events into routine experiences that generate manageable stress levels. Beyond practicing physical maneuvers, preparation includes oral examination rehearsals covering aerodynamic principles, aircraft systems, regulations, weather theory, and scenario-based decision-making questions. Examiners probe understanding rather than accepting memorized responses, asking follow-up questions to determine whether students truly comprehend concepts or merely repeat textbook phrases. This intellectual examination challenges students to articulate clearly what they know, explaining concepts in their own words and applying theoretical knowledge to practical scenarios. The preparation process reveals knowledge gaps requiring study and builds confidence through demonstrated competence, removing doubt about readiness. On examination day, prepared students approach the event with appropriate respect but without debilitating anxiety, knowing their training has equipped them with the skills and knowledge necessary for success.

The journey toward checkride completion represents far more than satisfying regulatory requirements for pilot certification. These maneuvers and procedures constitute the vocabulary of airmanship, the fundamental language through which pilots communicate with their aircraft and the environment. Steep turns teach energy management and loading effects applicable throughout aviation careers. Slow flight develops the edge-of-envelope awareness necessary for safe landing operations. Stall training builds the reflexes that prevent loss-of-control accidents. Ground reference maneuvers develop the wind-correction skills essential for visual navigation. Emergency procedures establish the mental discipline needed to respond effectively during crises. Each element contributes to the comprehensive skill set that defines competent pilots, building layers of capability that eventually coalesce into genuine airmanship. Students often fail to appreciate this progression while immersed in training details, focusing on passing examinations rather than recognizing how individual lessons integrate into professional capability. Yet looking backward after certification reveals the deliberate architecture underlying training sequences, showing how instructors systematically constructed knowledge and skill foundations, then built upon them progressively until students could operate safely across diverse conditions. The investment of time, money, and effort required to reach checkride readiness pays dividends throughout a flying career because these fundamentals never become obsolete. Commercial pilots fly steep turns while maneuvering for photographs, instrument pilots use slow flight skills during approach procedures, and airline captains apply emergency response discipline when managing system failures on international flights. The maneuvers mastered during private pilot training echo forward through all subsequent aviation experiences, their lessons deepening with experience but remaining fundamentally unchanged. The clouds themselves remain eternally beyond reach despite humanity's technological achievements in navigating them. Still, pilots who master these essential maneuvers gain the skills necessary to safely explore the sky's infinite possibilities, transforming dreams of flight into routine realities accomplished with confidence and competence earned through dedicated practice and disciplined training.

Chapter 6: Weathering the Storm: Understanding Meteorology

The atmosphere that supports flight simultaneously presents aviation's most unpredictable challenges, a vast three-dimensional ocean of air whose invisible currents, pressures, and moisture content dictate whether dreams take wing or remain grounded. Unlike mechanical systems that operate according to predictable engineering principles or navigation techniques that rely on mathematical certainty, weather is a dynamic, ever-changing force that demands respect, understanding, and conservative decision-making from pilots at every level of experience. The transition from relying on instructor judgment to making personal weather assessments represents one of training's most critical evolutions, requiring knowledge that extends far beyond simple cloud identification or wind speed interpretation. Aviation meteorology encompasses understanding atmospheric physics, pressure systems, frontal boundaries, visibility restrictions, icing conditions, thunderstorm development, and the countless subtle indicators that experienced pilots learn to recognize through years of careful observation combined with formal study.

The fundamental concept underlying all aviation meteorology is that weather results from differential heating of Earth's surface by solar radiation, creating temperature gradients that generate wind, pressure variations, and moisture redistribution across vast geographic scales. Equatorial regions receive more concentrated solar energy than polar areas, establishing the fundamental heat imbalance that drives global circulation patterns. Land surfaces heat and cool more rapidly than water bodies, creating distinct temperature differences between coastal and inland areas that produce predictable wind patterns during different times of day. Mountains force air upward, triggering cooling that may produce clouds and precipitation on windward slopes while creating drier conditions on leeward sides. These fundamental processes operate continuously, interacting in complex ways that determine the specific weather conditions pilots encounter during each flight. Understanding these underlying mechanisms transforms weather observation from passive acceptance of conditions into active interpretation of atmospheric processes, allowing pilots to anticipate changes, recognize developing hazards, and make informed decisions about flight safety. The atmosphere reveals its intentions through observable signs for those trained to interpret them, providing warnings about deteriorating conditions long before danger becomes immediate.

Pressure systems form the backbone of weather pattern organization, with areas of relatively high and low atmospheric pressure creating the circulation patterns that move weather across continents and oceans. High-pressure systems, technically called anticyclones, feature descending air that warms as it compresses, typically producing stable atmospheric conditions with clear skies and good visibility. Air circulates clockwise around high-pressure centers in the Northern Hemisphere, flowing outward from the center in a diverging pattern that generally creates favorable flying weather. Pilots planning cross-country flights actively seek routes that keep them within high-pressure influence, knowing that such systems typically provide smooth air, unrestricted visibility, and minimal turbulence. Low-pressure systems, or cyclones, feature rising air that cools as it expands, creating instability that generates clouds, precipitation, and generally unfavorable flight conditions. Air circulates counterclockwise around low-pressure centers in the Northern Hemisphere, converging toward the center where upward motion carries moisture aloft to form weather systems ranging from gentle rain showers to severe thunderstorms. The movement of these pressure systems follows somewhat predictable patterns influenced by upper-level winds, allowing meteorologists to forecast weather trends several days in advance with reasonable accuracy for flight planning purposes.

Frontal systems mark the boundaries between air masses with different temperature and moisture characteristics, creating zones of enhanced weather activity that demand particular attention from pilots planning flights. Cold fronts occur when advancing cold air masses undercut warmer air ahead, forcing rapid upward motion that produces towering cumulus clouds, possible thunderstorms, gusty surface winds, and marked temperature drops following frontal passage. The steep frontal slope characteristic of cold fronts concentrates weather activity into relatively narrow bands, typically extending 50 to 100 miles ahead of the surface frontal boundary. Pilots monitoring weather for cross-country flights learn to recognize cold front signatures on weather charts and satellite imagery, understanding that attempting to fly through active cold fronts exposes aircraft to severe turbulence, icing, reduced visibility, and dangerous wind shear near the surface. The prudent decision is to wait for frontal passage, after which high pressure typically builds behind the front, creating the excellent flying weather that follows cold front systems. Warm fronts form when advancing warm air overruns retreating cold air, creating a gradual upward motion along a shallow frontal slope that extends hundreds of miles ahead of the surface boundary. This gentle lifting produces layered cloud systems that progressively lower toward the surface as the front approaches, creating extended periods of reduced visibility, low ceilings, and persistent precipitation that may present instrument meteorological conditions unsuitable for visual flight operations.

Visibility restrictions challenge pilots more immediately than many other weather phenomena because flight under visual flight rules requires maintaining specific minimum distances from clouds and minimum flight visibility for legal operation. Haze results from suspended particles, including dust, smoke, and industrial pollutants, which scatter light and reduce contrast, making it challenging to distinguish ground features or other aircraft at a distance. Flying in haze creates illusions about actual visibility conditions, as looking downward toward the surface may reveal reasonable clarity while horizontal visibility remains severely restricted. Pilots caught in haze often find themselves in disorienting situations in which familiar landmarks disappear, distances become difficult to judge accurately, and other aircraft remain invisible until they are dangerously close. Fog represents an even more serious visibility restriction, forming when air temperature drops to the dew point temperature, causing water vapor to condense into tiny droplets suspended near the surface. Radiation fog develops during clear, calm nights as the ground radiates heat into space, cooling the adjacent air layer to saturation. This fog type typically forms after midnight, deepens toward dawn, and dissipates within hours after sunrise as solar heating warms the air above the condensation point. Pilots planning early morning flights must carefully monitor the temperature-dew point spread the previous evening, recognizing that spreads of three degrees or less indicate a high probability of radiation fog development that could trap aircraft on the ground or create hazardous landing conditions.

Advection fog forms when warm, moist air moves over cooler surfaces, lowering the air temperature to its dew point through contact cooling rather than through radiation. Coastal areas frequently experience advection fog when maritime air moves onshore across cooler land surfaces, creating persistent fog that may last for days regardless of time or solar heating. This fog type particularly challenges pilots because it forms unpredictably, moves with wind patterns, and resists dissipation through regular diurnal heating cycles. Many coastal airports remain unusable for extended periods when advection fog settles over their locations, stranding aircraft and canceling planned flights until wind patterns shift to bring drier air masses. Upslope fog develops when moist air flows up gradually rising terrain, cooling adiabatically as it grows until it reaches saturation. The Great Plains region experiences upslope fog when easterly winds carry Gulf moisture westward against the gradually rising terrain, creating fog that may extend across multiple states and persist for extended periods. Understanding these different fog formation mechanisms helps pilots interpret current observations and forecast discussions, recognize situations where fog development is likely, and plan alternative arrangements accordingly, rather than launch flights that are likely to encounter visibility restrictions below safe minimums.

Thunderstorms represent aviation's most dramatic and dangerous weather phenomena, posing hazards such as severe turbulence, hail, icing, lightning, and violent wind shear that can destroy aircraft attempting to penetrate them. Every thunderstorm passes through identifiable stages that reflect its lifecycle from initial development through maturity to eventual dissipation. The cumulus stage features strong updrafts that build towering clouds at rates potentially exceeding 6,000 feet per minute, carrying moisture to high altitudes where freezing creates precipitation particles. No precipitation falls during this initial stage, but the rapidly building cloud presents severe turbulence hazards to any aircraft venturing nearby. The mature stage begins when precipitation becomes sufficiently heavy to create downdrafts within the storm, establishing the characteristic circulation pattern with updrafts and downdrafts existing simultaneously. This stage produces the most severe weather, including heavy rain, hail, and lightning, and possibly tornadoes if conditions are favorable for their development. Pilots absolutely must avoid mature thunderstorms by wide margins, recognizing that turbulence extends far beyond visible cloud boundaries and that storm cells may intensify rapidly without warning. The dissipating stage occurs when downdrafts dominate throughout the storm, cutting off the updraft supply that sustained development. Precipitation weakens, cloud tops begin spreading into anvil shapes, and severe weather gradually diminishes, though significant turbulence may persist even in dissipating storms.

Thunderstorm varieties range from isolated airmass storms that develop during summer afternoons to organized squall lines extending hundreds of miles and containing numerous severe cells. Airmass thunderstorms typically form when solar heating creates instability in moist air masses, triggering updrafts that build into isolated storms scattered across vast areas. These storms generally remain stationary or move slowly, following the wind pattern in which they formed. While individual airmass storms may produce severe weather, pilots can usually circumnavigate them with reasonable deviations, maintaining visual contact with storm cells and avoiding areas of visible precipitation and dark cloud bases. Frontal thunderstorms develop along cold front boundaries where strong lifting mechanisms combine with abundant moisture and instability to create lines of storms potentially hundreds of miles long. These organized systems may contain supercell storms with rotating updrafts that spawn tornadoes, produce baseball-sized hail, and generate damaging straight-line winds extending far beyond precipitation areas. Pilots encountering frontal thunderstorm lines face difficult decisions, as deviating around extensive squall lines may require hundreds of additional miles of flight or precautionary landings to wait for the system to pass. The conservative choice always involves landing and waiting rather than attempting penetration or flying beneath storm bases where wind shear and turbulence create extreme hazards.

Icing conditions pose particularly insidious threats because ice accumulation progressively degrades aircraft performance, adding weight and disrupting aerodynamic surfaces until flight becomes impossible to sustain. Structural icing forms when supercooled water droplets strike aircraft surfaces and freeze on contact, building ice formations that increase weight, reduce lift, increase drag, and potentially jam control surfaces. The icing environment exists in clouds, where temperatures range from 0 to -20 degrees Celsius, creating conditions in which water droplets remain liquid even at below-freezing temperatures. Not all clouds produce icing; frigid temperatures create ice-crystal clouds that pass harmlessly around aircraft surfaces. Still, pilots cannot visually distinguish between ice crystal clouds and supercooled droplet clouds before entering them. Rime ice forms when small droplets freeze rapidly on contact, creating rough, opaque ice that builds forward into the relative wind. Clear ice develops when large droplets flow backward before freezing, creating smooth, transparent ice that adheres firmly to surfaces and proves extremely difficult to remove. Mixed ice combines characteristics of both types, creating particularly problematic accumulations that severely affect aircraft performance. Training aircraft lack ice-protection systems beyond pitot heat, making any icing encounter potentially catastrophic as accumulation continues without a means to remove it.

Understanding icing threats requires careful attention to temperature profiles, cloud types, and moisture content throughout planned flight routes. Pilots must analyze forecast freezing levels, current pilot reports, and surface weather observations to identify areas where icing conditions exist or may develop. The presence of precipitation, combined with near-freezing surface temperatures, strongly suggests icing aloft, as freezing rain and ice pellet observations indicate that supercooled droplets are present in clouds above. Frontal systems frequently create icing conditions as warm air overruns cold surface air, producing stratiform clouds with sustained moisture content through deep atmospheric layers. Pilots caught in unexpected icing must act decisively to escape conditions before accumulation becomes critical, changing altitude to find temperatures above freezing or below the supercooled droplet range, or immediately landing at the nearest suitable airport if escape proves impossible. The conservative approach avoids filing flight plans that require flying through forecast icing conditions, recognizing that training aircraft lack equipment for safe icing penetration and that even brief exposure may create hazardous situations. Many experienced pilots maintain personal minimums more restrictive than regulations require, refusing to fly when the temperature-dew point spread suggests possible cloud formation and temperatures hover near freezing levels, understanding that theoretical icing potential warrants avoiding marginal conditions entirely.

Wind patterns at various altitudes significantly affect flight planning, influencing groundspeed, fuel consumption, and the time required to complete planned routes. Surface winds primarily concern pilots during takeoff and landing operations, as crosswind components challenge directional control, while headwinds and tailwinds affect the length of the runway needed for safe operations. Winds aloft are crucial for cross-country flight planning: headwinds slow progress and increase fuel consumption, while tailwinds provide essentially free groundspeed increases that may substantially reduce flight time. Wind direction and velocity typically increase with altitude due to reduced friction, creating stronger winds at higher altitudes where most cross-country flights operate. The winds aloft forecasts published by aviation weather services provide predicted wind directions and speeds at various altitudes every three hours, allowing pilots to select altitudes that optimize groundspeed for their planned routes. Flying from west to east generally benefits from the prevailing westerly winds, while eastbound flights face headwind penalties that lengthen flight times and consume additional fuel. Competent pilots incorporate winds aloft analysis into flight planning, sometimes choosing less direct routes that angle away from straight-line courses to take advantage of more favorable wind components that ultimately provide faster overall progress toward destination airports.

Mountain wave activity creates atmospheric conditions that produce extraordinary turbulence and vertical currents strong enough to exceed aircraft climb capability, presenting hazards that extend far downwind from visible mountain ranges. When stable air flows across mountain barriers with wind speeds exceeding twenty-five knots, the terrain forces air upward along windward slopes before accelerating downward on leeward sides, creating oscillating wave patterns that extend vertically to great altitudes and horizontally for hundreds of miles downwind. Lenticular clouds, smooth lens-shaped formations that appear stationary despite strong winds, mark areas where wave crests reach condensation levels. Rotor clouds —ragged, turbulent clouds that form beneath wave crests —indicate hazardous turbulence areas where vertical and horizontal wind shear combine to create conditions capable of overstressing aircraft structures. Mountain wave rotors have destroyed aircraft attempting flight in their vicinity, with survivors describing violence beyond any turbulence previously experienced. Cap clouds draping smoothly over mountain peaks indicate active wave conditions that warrant avoiding flight operations near affected ranges. Pilots planning flights near mountainous terrain must carefully examine current weather patterns for wind directions perpendicular to prominent ridgelines, combined with speeds suggesting wave development, then either cancel flights or route well clear of affected areas to avoid unintentional wave encounters.

Density altitude calculations are critical for performance planning, particularly when operating from high-elevation airports on warm days, when reduced air density significantly degrades aircraft performance. Density altitude represents pressure altitude corrected for nonstandard temperature, providing a measurement that reflects the actual air density at a given altitude. High density altitude means thin air that produces less engine power, reduces propeller efficiency, and decreases wing lift generation, resulting in longer takeoff rolls, reduced climb rates, and potentially the inability to clear obstacles during departure. A sea-level airport on a standard temperature day produces a density altitude equal to field elevation. Still, the same airport on a very hot day might experience a density altitude thousands of feet higher than actual elevation. Mountain airports at high actual elevations compound these effects, as the combination of high elevation and warm temperatures can create density altitudes exceeding 10,000 feet, where naturally aspirated engines produce perhaps 65% of sea-level power. Pilots trained at sea-level airports sometimes fail to appreciate density-altitude effects until attempting mountain airport operations, discovering that familiar aircraft performance is dramatically different when air density decreases significantly. Computing density altitude before every flight becomes an essential habit, particularly during summer months when high temperatures combine with barometric pressure variations to create reduced performance conditions even at relatively low elevations.

Weather information sources have expanded dramatically through technological advancement, providing pilots with comprehensive meteorological data accessible through multiple channels before and during flight operations. Aviation routine weather reports, known as METARs, present encoded current weather observations from airports equipped with weather reporting capability, updating hourly with special reports issued when significant changes occur between scheduled observations. Terminal aerodrome forecasts, abbreviated as TAFs, provide predicted weather conditions at specific airports, covering periods of 18 to 30 hours into the future, offering essential planning information on expected ceiling heights, visibility, wind patterns, and precipitation. Area forecasts describe expected weather across broad geographic regions, highlighting significant meteorological features such as frontal systems, pressure patterns, icing conditions, and turbulence. Graphical weather products, including surface analysis charts, radar summaries, satellite imagery, and forecast charts, provide visual representations that help pilots understand current conditions and predicted developments across their planned routes. Flight service stations staffed by specialists trained in aviation weather interpretation offer comprehensive preflight briefings that combine all available weather information into coherent pictures of expected conditions, highlighting factors relevant to planned flights and recommending alternatives when weather appears marginal or unsuitable for safe operations.

Modern technology delivers weather information through internet-connected devices, enabling pilots to access comprehensive meteorological data through dedicated aviation weather websites, tablet applications, and smartphone interfaces. These digital resources present the same official weather products that professionals use, in user-friendly displays that simplify interpretation and highlight relevant information for specific flight-planning needs. Real-time radar imagery shows precipitation intensity and coverage, updating every few minutes to reveal the movement and development of weather systems. Satellite imagery provides broad-scale views of cloud coverage, storm systems, and frontal boundaries across continents. Graphical forecast products overlay predicted weather elements onto geographic maps, illustrating how conditions may evolve over the coming hours. Pilot reports submitted by aircraft already flying along planned routes offer ground truth about actual conditions encountered, providing invaluable information about turbulence levels, icing reports, cloud tops and bases, visibility conditions, and wind variations that forecasts may not capture accurately. In-flight weather services available through portable devices equipped with ADS-B receivers provide cockpit access to real-time weather updates, enabling en route decision-making based on current conditions rather than preflight briefing information that may be hours old.

Personal weather minimums establish conservative standards that account for experience levels, aircraft capability, and individual comfort with various meteorological conditions, typically exceeding regulatory minimums by substantial margins. Regulations specify minimum visibility and cloud clearance requirements for visual flight operations. Still, these legal minimums often prove inadequate for pilots with limited experience or unfamiliarity with specific geographic areas. Establishing personal minimums might involve requiring three thousand-foot ceilings and five miles of visibility for cross-country flights, even though regulations permit one thousand-foot ceilings and three miles of visibility in controlled airspace. Nighttime operations warrant higher minimums than daytime flights, as reduced visual references combine with darkness to create disorientation risks when weather deteriorates unexpectedly. Mountain flying demands particularly conservative minimums given limited emergency landing options and terrain-induced turbulence, wind patterns, and rapid weather changes characteristic of mountainous regions. Crosswind limitations based on demonstrated proficiency rather than aircraft capability prevent attempts to land beyond comfortable skill levels when wind conditions challenge directional control. These personal standards evolve throughout flying careers as experience builds and proficiency increases, but maintaining conservative minimums prevents accidents caused by pushing beyond current capability or attempting flight in conditions beyond safe parameters.

The go-no-go decision is the most critical judgment pilots make, weighing multiple weather factors against aircraft capability, personal proficiency, and flight necessity to determine whether proceeding is safe and reasonable. This decision-making process begins during initial flight planning when reviewing forecasts and current conditions for departure, en route, and destination areas. Marginal weather at any point along the planned route warrants careful evaluation, considering whether conditions might deteriorate further, whether suitable alternate airports exist if weather becomes unacceptable, and whether delaying the flight might provide improved conditions. Pilots sometimes face subtle pressure to complete flights despite marginal weather, particularly when passengers await transport, business obligations create urgency, or personal schedules demand adherence to planned timelines. Resisting such pressure requires discipline and recognition that weather-related accidents frequently involve continuation decisions made despite deteriorating conditions that should have triggered immediate landings. The professional approach treats every flight as optional, regardless of schedule pressures, and cancels or postpones operations when weather poses unacceptable risk. Building experience through conservative decision-making establishes judgment patterns that protect against the accident sequence in which marginal conditions gradually worsen until escape becomes impossible, and tragedy results from decisions made incrementally rather than deliberately choosing unsafe operations.

Aviation meteorology extends beyond technical knowledge into developing weather wisdom, the intuitive understanding that grows from years of observing atmospheric behavior, correlating forecasts with actual conditions, and recognizing subtle patterns that indicate developing situations before obvious signs appear. This wisdom accumulates through deliberate practice of weather observation, examining sky conditions daily regardless of flying plans, noting relationships between pressure trends and weather changes, and maintaining personal weather records that document local patterns throughout seasonal cycles. Experienced pilots develop an almost subconscious weather sense that triggers caution when conditions appear superficially acceptable but subtle indicators suggest potential problems. They notice thickening haze that might transition into instrument conditions, recognize cloud formations that precede thunderstorm development, and detect wind pattern changes suggesting a frontal approach before weather services issue advisories. This developed sense combines formal meteorological knowledge with practical experience, creating judgment that serves throughout aviation careers. Student pilots beginning this weather education journey benefit from approaching meteorology not as an academic requirement but as essential survival knowledge requiring ongoing study and practical application. The atmosphere reveals its intentions through observable evidence, rewarding those who learn its language with safe passage through ever-changing sky conditions that make each flight unique while demanding respect for forces far beyond human control.

Chapter 7: Cross-Country Adventures: Expanding Horizons

The cockpit feels different when the destination lies beyond the horizon, when familiar training patterns give way to purposeful journeys that stretch across state lines and time zones. Cross-country flying represents a fundamental transformation in pilot development, shifting the perspective from aircraft operation within known confines to genuine navigation across unfamiliar territories, where decision-making, resource management, and situational awareness reach entirely new dimensions. Federal Aviation Regulations define cross-country flight as any journey exceeding 50 nautical miles from the original departure point. Yet, this bureaucratic definition fails to capture the psychological threshold crossed when pilots commit to flights in which turning back requires deliberation rather than instinct. The sectional chart spread across your lap transforms from an academic reference to an essential lifeline, connecting your present position with your intended destination across hundreds of miles of terrain. Towns and cities marked as small circles on paper become three-dimensional realities requiring identification from altitude, their unique patterns of roads, water features, and prominent landmarks confirming navigation accuracy or revealing disorienting course deviations. This expanded operational scope introduces complexity layering far beyond pattern work and practice areas, demanding integration of skills previously practiced in isolation into a comprehensive aviation competency where pilotage, dead reckoning, radio navigation, communication, fuel management, weather assessment, and aeronautical decision-making converge into continuous operational demands that allow no mental respite during multi-hour journeys.

Planning the first extended cross-country flight requires a mental shift from routine practice missions to genuine expedition preparation, where the consequences of poor judgment amplify with distance from home base. The process begins days before engine start, examining charts spanning hundreds of square miles to select routes that balance directness with practical considerations unavailable to simple point-to-point straight lines drawn with rulers. Terrain elevation requires careful attention where mountain ridges interrupt valleys, their heights demanding flight altitudes that account for safety margins while respecting aircraft performance limitations at density altitudes where summer heat thins air and reduces climb capability. Airspace complexity increases dramatically when courses traverse multiple terminal areas, military operations zones, and restricted regions requiring either circumnavigation or specific communication procedures for penetration. The chart becomes covered with pencil marks as pilots plot checkpoints approximately every ten to fifteen miles along the proposed route, selecting distinctive ground features recognizable from typical cruising altitudes where perspective compresses details into abstract patterns. Water towers, highway intersections, distinctive lakes, railway junctions, and prominent elevation changes become vital references confirming position during flight when electronic devices might fail or provide ambiguous information. Each checkpoint receives a notation with the magnetic heading, estimated time between points, and cumulative distance traveled, transforming abstract geography into actionable navigation data usable during flight when workload prevents complex calculations. Weather forecasts receive scrutiny that extends beyond simple go/no-go assessments into detailed analysis examining conditions along the entire route and at the destination, with particular attention to expected arrival-time conditions that might deteriorate while en route, trapping pilots in situations where safe return options evaporate behind advancing fronts or lowering ceilings.

Fuel planning introduces variables absent from local training flights, where airports always remain within gliding distance and reserve margins remain comfortably large. Cross-country flights demand precise calculations accounting for cruise consumption rates, winds aloft that accelerate or diminish groundspeed against headwind components, and reserve requirements to ensure adequate margins for diversions, weather delays, or navigation errors that extend intended routes. Conservative pilots calculate fuel requirements using worst-case scenarios in which headwinds exceed forecasts and consumption exceeds manufacturers' optimistic specifications, then add additional reserves beyond regulatory minimums, recognizing that fuel in wing tanks provides options. In contrast, fuel in underground storage offers only regret when shortages materialize overhead, in unfamiliar territory. The mathematics becomes personal rather than academic when pilots consider that fuel exhaustion remains among aviation's most preventable emergencies, yet continues to claim aircraft and lives with disturbing regularity, often due to optimistic planning combined with reluctance to adjust plans when conditions change in-flight. Weight and balance calculations take on renewed importance when full fuel loads are combined with passengers and baggage approaching the maximum gross weight, requiring pilots to verify that planned destinations feature runway lengths adequate for landing distances that increase dramatically when aircraft arrive heavy at high-density-altitude airports, where afternoon heat degrades performance. These practical considerations force decisions between carrying additional fuel weight and reducing passenger loads, between direct routes and longer paths that avoid high terrain, and between ambitious schedules and conservative alternatives that sacrifice efficiency for enhanced safety margins.

Filing flight plans represents an operational milestone at which student pilots transition from closely supervised trainees to independent operators, declaring intentions to the national aviation system and accepting responsibility for following through on commitments, barring genuine emergencies or weather deterioration necessitating alternate actions. The flight plan form, whether submitted electronically or via telephone briefing, provides search and rescue services with critical information should an aircraft fail to arrive within a reasonable time after its estimated arrival, triggering searches that can mean the difference between survival and tragedy when forced landings occur in remote areas. Beyond this safety function, flight plans impose helpful discipline on planning processes, requiring pilots to formalize route selections, altitude choices, and fuel calculations in concrete terms, subject to review by others, rather than leaving vague intentions open to impulsive modification. The act of filing creates psychological commitment, reducing the temptation to make casual course deviations or to rationalize poor decisions as minor variations from original plans. Activating flight plans after departure involves a simple radio call to Flight Service or an automated system. Yet, surprisingly many pilots file plans without activating them, negating the safety benefits entirely. Equally important, closing flight plans upon arrival prevents unnecessary searches when aircraft land safely but pilots forget or neglect this final communication responsibility, creating false emergencies that waste search resources while undermining system effectiveness.

Departure day arrives with heightened awareness that every action carries amplified significance beyond familiar pattern operations. The preflight inspection receives additional scrutiny, with fluid levels, control surfaces, tire pressure, and fuel quantity checked with greater diligence, recognizing that mechanical issues that develop during long flights can present complications absent during local training. The amount of fuel visible during preflight receives verification against fuel receipts and expected levels rather than a casual assumption that tanks were serviced correctly, as fuel exhaustion accidents frequently involve erroneous assumptions about the quantity available. Weather is reviewed immediately before departure rather than relying solely on morning briefings, as atmospheric conditions change continuously and last-minute deterioration might warrant postponement despite perfect forecasts hours earlier. This final weather check cultivates habits that distinguish cautious pilots from those who rationalize proceeding despite warning signs, developing judgment that separates acceptable risk from foolhardy optimism, a factor that statistical analyses repeatedly identify as a factor in preventable accidents. The engine run-up proceeds through familiar steps, but with recognition that extended operations demand absolute confidence in powerplant reliability; any hesitation, unusual indication, or uncertain response warrants ground investigation rather than airborne discovery over remote terrain. Radio communications with clearance delivery or ground control formalize departure intentions, inserting the flight into the organized traffic flow while establishing initial contact with air traffic services that assist in the journey.

Lifting off into an extended cross-country flight generates a sensation distinctly different from routine training departures circling back to familiar airports. The initial climb away from the airport environment continues beyond typical practice area altitudes, reaching cruise altitude where the horizon expands across fifty or more miles of visible terrain, depending on atmospheric clarity and elevation. The throttle setting stabilizes at cruise power after climb, the engine settling into a steady rhythm that will continue for hours rather than minutes, its reliable operation becoming background awareness monitored through periodic instrument scans rather than constant attention. The first checkpoint approaches within minutes, offering immediate feedback on navigation accuracy: the actual ground track either confirms the planned course or reveals deviations that require correction before errors compound over accumulated miles. Identifying checkpoints from altitude develops skills quite distinct from chart reading on the ground, as three-dimensional landmarks compress into two-dimensional patterns, where perspective, scale, and intervening obscurations challenge recognition. Towns that appear substantial on charts might present as barely distinguishable clusters of buildings from cruising altitude. At the same time, prominent features such as distinctive lake shapes or highway intersections provide unmistakable confirmation even when the surrounding terrain differs from what was anticipated. The mental discipline of continuously tracking position prevents the insidious drift into vague awareness, where pilots maintain a general sense of location without precise knowledge. This dangerous habit leaves them lost and unaware that they are disoriented until errors become severe. This positional awareness involves marking estimated position on charts every few minutes, noting the time over identified checkpoints, and calculating whether groundspeed matches preflight predictions or reveals wind effects requiring heading adjustments to maintain the desired ground track.

Radio frequency changes occur regularly as the flight progresses across airspace boundaries, transitioning from departure control to en route frequencies to approach control serving destination areas, each contact requiring standard phraseology and aircraft identification while monitoring traffic information affecting the intended flight path. Communication during cross-country flight lacks the familiar comfort of local operations, where controllers recognize training aircraft and student voices become known through repetition. Instead, pilots enter airspace servicing hundreds of transient aircraft daily, where controllers maintain professional efficiency while managing complex traffic flows largely invisible to individual pilots operating under Visual Flight Rules. This environment demands clear, confident communication, despite knowing that experienced commercial pilots use the same frequencies, and it helps overcome the natural intimidation that can cause some student pilots to avoid communication or use uncertain tones that undermine professionalism. The radio discipline developed during cross-country operations serves throughout aviation careers, establishing communication habits that convey competence while obtaining necessary services and information, enhancing safety and efficiency. Flight-following services from air traffic control provide significant benefits during cross-country operations, offering radar monitoring that alerts pilots to traffic conflicts and ready assistance should weather or mechanical issues arise. These services, available upon request but not mandatory for VFR operations, provide free insurance against situations where immediate help or local knowledge becomes valuable. Yet surprisingly many pilots decline them due to misguided self-sufficiency or reluctance to accept traffic advisories that require radio communication.

Fuel management transitions from abstract planning to concrete monitoring as flights progress and tanks gradually drain toward reserve levels. The fuel gauges, often notoriously inaccurate in small aircraft, receive correlation with calculated consumption rates based on elapsed time and known fuel flow rates, providing reasonable estimates of remaining endurance. Conservative pilots avoid stretching fuel to the theoretical limits; instead, they plan fuel stops with comfortable margins that prevent anxiety-inducing calculations about whether the remaining fuel suffices for the destination and required reserves. The psychology of fuel awareness introduces decision-making pressures in which schedule demands conflict with prudent margins, in which pilots convince themselves that forecast tailwinds will materialize despite contrary groundspeed evidence, or in which ego prevents acknowledging navigation errors that extend routes beyond planned distances. These human factors account for continued fuel exhaustion accidents despite universal training emphasizing adequate reserves and despite fuel availability at airports scattered throughout most regions. The discipline of setting personal minimums regarding fuel reserves, perhaps requiring landing with one hour remaining rather than regulatory minimums, creates margins that accommodate unexpected headwinds, diversions around weather, or navigation inefficiencies without approaching critical situations. Flights requiring fuel stops introduce additional planning considerations for airport selection, including fuel availability, runway conditions, approaches suitable for the pilot's experience level, and services available in case of delays or issues.

En route, weather assessment becomes a critical skill as flights approach destinations where conditions might deviate from forecast expectations. The sky ahead is continuously scanned for cloud buildups suggesting convective activity, reduced visibility indicating approaching frontal systems, or ceilings lowering, threatening continued VFR operations. Weather deviations during cross-country flight require far more complex decision-making than local operations, where familiar airports remain accessible within minutes. Pilots must evaluate whether current conditions permit continued flight toward destinations, whether alternate routes around weather systems remain feasible within fuel reserves, whether intermediate airports offer suitable landing options, or whether prudent action dictates an immediate diversion regardless of schedule pressures or passenger expectations. This real-time meteorological decision-making separates pilots who demonstrate genuine judgment from those who rationalize continuing into deteriorating conditions, hoping circumstances will improve before they become critical. Visual flight rules impose clear weather minimums for visibility and cloud clearances, yet accidents repeatedly demonstrate that legal minima are often insufficient for safe operations when conditions approach those limits. The VFR pilot encountering marginal conditions faces powerful psychological pressures toward continuation, having invested significant time and resources reaching the current position, with the destination tantalizingly near and passengers expecting arrival. Yet statistics unambiguously demonstrate that VFR flight into instrument meteorological conditions remains among aviation's most lethal scenarios, typically proving fatal within minutes of cloud entry due to disorientation. The discipline of establishing conservative personal weather minimums well above regulatory requirements, perhaps declining to continue when ceilings drop below 3,000 feet or visibility falls below 5 miles, creates margins that prevent pilots from reaching decision points at which continuing and retreating both present unacceptable risks.

Navigation error recognition and correction is an essential skill during cross-country operations, where courses extending across hundreds of miles can cause minor heading errors to produce substantial position deviations over time. The classic one-degree heading error produces approximately one mile lateral displacement per sixty miles traveled, meaning that course deviations as small as five degrees result in aircraft positioned nearly ten miles off-course after just two hours of flight. These errors compound when pilots fail to recognize deviations promptly, instead maintaining incorrect headings while assuming navigation remains accurate. The checkpoint system provides critical error detection: the absence or unrecognizability of ground features at expected times signals navigation discrepancies that require immediate investigation. Discovering oneself off-course generates understandable concern, yet this situation demands calm analysis rather than panicked responses that worsen disorientation. The proper response involves admitting uncertainty, flying a specific heading while maintaining altitude, and systematically working to reestablish position through deliberate ground-feature identification, radio navigation assistance, or communication with air traffic control to request assistance. Pride prevents many pilots from acknowledging confusion until situations deteriorate seriously. In contrast, experienced aviators recognize that occasional navigation uncertainty affects everyone and that prompt corrective action prevents minor confusion from escalating into a genuine emergency. Modern portable GPS devices and electronic flight bag applications provide powerful navigation assistance that dramatically reduces the workload of traditional pilotage and dead reckoning. Yet, regulations wisely require pilots to demonstrate navigation competency without electronic assistance, recognizing that technology failures could occur when clouds obscure ground features or when confusion about device operation introduces errors potentially more dangerous than traditional methods.

Arriving at destination airports after multi-hour cross-country flights generates satisfaction quite distinct from countless pattern landings at familiar home bases. The airport environment appears completely fresh, lacking the intimate familiarity with runway features, traffic patterns, noise abatement procedures, and local geographical references that make home-base operations almost automatic. Pilots must locate the airport relative to the current track, typically first identifying the general area from distance, then systematically scanning for runway surfaces that blend surprisingly well with the surrounding terrain. The Automated Surface Observing System broadcast provides current winds, altimeter setting, and active runway information, essential for planning appropriate pattern entry. However, interpreting this information correctly requires understanding local procedures that may differ from familiar home-based practices. Some airports use left-hand traffic patterns for all runways, while others use right-hand traffic patterns for specific runways to avoid populated areas or terrain conflicts. Non-towered fields might host pilots using non-standard entries despite published procedures. This uncertainty demands enhanced vigilance during arrival phases, when multiple aircraft may converge simultaneously, with some pilots clearly announcing their positions. In contrast, others remain silent, assuming that visual scanning alone suffices for conflict avoidance. Position reports on Common Traffic Advisory Frequency follow standard formats announcing aircraft identification, position relative to the airport, altitude, and intentions, creating shared situational awareness among pilots operating in the uncontrolled environment. The pattern entry itself requires extra concentration compared to familiar operations, judging appropriate distances for downwind legs, turning base leg at proper positions, and managing descent and approach speeds that vary with unfamiliar surroundings lacking customary visual references. The landing demands full attention as threshold height assessment occurs without a familiar perspective, requiring trust in instrument indications and fundamental airspeed control rather than visual cues that develop only through repeated operations at specific locations.

Post-flight procedures at destination airports introduce practical considerations absent from home base operations, where support and resources remain familiar. Securing the aircraft requires finding appropriate tie-down locations, obtaining permission to park, and ensuring the airplane remains protected from the weather and security concerns for however long the visit continues. Fuel arrangements receive attention when extended return flights require full tanks. However, pilots must verify whether self-service fuel systems are available or whether attended service operates on limited schedules that might not accommodate desired departure times. Ground transportation often requires planning, since many smaller airports lack rental car services or taxi availability common at larger facilities, leaving pilots sometimes stranded miles from intended destinations without practical means to cover the final distances. These mundane logistics receive insufficient emphasis during training. Yet, they frequently create complications that diminish the enjoyment of cross-country flights while teaching valuable lessons about comprehensive planning that extends beyond flight operations into complete journey considerations. The return flight, whether immediate or following overnight stays, begins the planning cycle anew with weather assessment, route selection, and preflight preparation adapted to current circumstances rather than original planning done days earlier. Some pilots discover that return journeys prove more challenging than outbound legs when afternoon heating generates turbulence and convective activity, when fatigue accumulates from earlier flying, or when pressure to return home creates subtle compromises in judgment that experienced aviators recognize and resist.

The long cross-country requirement for private pilot certification demands at least three points totaling over 300 nautical miles, with legs exceeding 50 nautical miles straight-line distance from each prior point, forcing students to orchestrate complex multi-destination flights that integrate all skills developed throughout training. This culminating navigation exercise transforms theoretical planning into practical application, where weather considerations, fuel management, communication procedures, and aeronautical decision-making co-occur across flights spanning entire days. Instructors accompany these first extended flights, observing student performance while guiding through unpredictable challenges that arise during extended operations. The experience reveals capabilities and limitations in ways impossible during local training, exposing how pilots manage workload when multiple demands compete for attention, how judgment operates when real consequences attach to decisions, and whether personality traits support safe operations or introduce risk factors requiring modification. Some students demonstrate impressive composure and systematic problem-solving under pressure, while others exhibit tendencies toward flustered responses, poor prioritization, or dangerous pride that prevent them from acknowledging uncertainty. These behavioral observations guide instructors in tailoring remaining training to address specific deficiencies while building on demonstrated strengths, personalizing instruction in ways a generic syllabus structure cannot. The solo cross-country flights that follow dual instruction represent genuine tests of independent capability where safety nets disappear and student pilots either demonstrate readiness for certification or reveal gaps requiring additional training before private pilot responsibilities become appropriate.

Cross-country flying develops perspectives impossible to appreciate through local operations alone, revealing aviation as a means of transportation rather than a recreational circle-flying, and exposing the genuine utility and freedom that attracted generations to pilot training. The ability to depart one's home area at dawn and arrive hundreds of miles distant in time for lunch, to visit remote locations unreachable by practical ground transportation, to view landscapes from perspectives impossible to observers confined to surface travel, these capabilities justify training investments and validate dreams that initiated the journey toward private pilot certification. Yet cross-country operations also expose aviation's limitations and demands, revealing that weather frequently dictates schedules rather than pilot desires, that careful planning and conservative judgment determine outcomes more than stick-and-rudder skills, and that every flight requires accepting responsibility for decisions affecting not merely personal safety but potentially passengers' lives and property on the ground beneath flight paths. This sobering maturity separates pilots who develop into safe, competent aviators from those who accumulate hours without gaining wisdom, who view regulations as annoying restrictions rather than distilled experience from tragedy, or who allow complacency to erode vigilance after familiarity breeds contempt for hazards requiring constant respect. The cross-country phase transforms student pilots into genuine aviators worthy of certification, expanding horizons literally and figuratively while developing judgment that makes the difference between long, satisfying aviation careers and premature finales recorded in accident statistics. The adventures embarked upon during this training phase create memories that last a lifetime while laying foundations for whatever aviation pursuits follow private pilot certification, whether recreational flying remains the goal or the private certificate becomes merely the first step toward professional aviation careers. The horizon continues to expand, limited only by a dedication to continuous learning and an unwavering commitment to the fundamental principles of safety, judgment, and professionalism that distinguish true aviators from mere airplane operators.

The psychological evolution occurring during cross-country operations extends beyond technical skill development into fundamental shifts in aeronautical perspective and self-perception. Student pilots begin training viewing themselves as learners practicing maneuvers under supervision, but cross-country flying transforms this identity into that of functioning aviators, making consequential decisions affecting real outcomes. This transition manifests in subtle behavioral changes: increased attention to weather forecasts days before flights, rather than casual glances at conditions; spontaneous mental calculations of winds aloft when planning weekend trips; and automatic scanning of sky conditions even when not flying. The airplane transforms from a training device into a practical means of transportation, prompting pilots to consider missions beyond practice flights: visiting distant friends, attending events in other cities, and exploring regions previously accessible only by tedious road travel. This expanding operational mindset brings aviation into daily life rather than keeping it compartmentalized to scheduled lessons.

The cross-country experience also cultivates humility regarding aviation's complexities and the continuous learning required for competent operations. Each flight presents unique combinations of conditions, challenges, and learning opportunities that prevent mastery despite accumulated experience. Weather behaves unexpectedly, navigation confusion occurs despite careful planning, communication misunderstandings arise despite clear intentions, and fatigue affects performance in ways not anticipated during planning phases. These humbling experiences teach that confidence must be balanced with caution, that admitting limitations demonstrates wisdom rather than weakness, and that aviation safety depends on recognizing that even experienced pilots encounter situations beyond their capabilities, requiring assistance, diversion, or cancellation. This mature perspective distinguishes dangerous overconfidence from healthy self-assurance, laying the foundation for safe flying throughout aviation careers spanning decades and thousands of flight hours beyond initial certification.

Chapter 8: The Art of Precision: Instrument Training

The fabric hood slides across the windscreen, transforming the familiar daytime world into a realm of partial vision where forward views disappear and only side windows remain visible. This simple device, reminiscent of a racing horse's blinders, creates the most disorienting training environment most private pilot students will encounter during their certification journey. The instructor's voice cuts through the sudden claustrophobia: "We're going to maintain straight and level flight using only your instruments. Keep your eyes inside the cockpit." The temptation to cheat — to glance through those side windows and steal visual references from the earth below — proves nearly overwhelming during these first moments under the hood. Yet this training represents something far more significant than an academic exercise in reading gauges; it introduces pilots to a fundamental truth about human perception and the absolute necessity of trusting objective instrumentation when subjective senses deceive. While private pilot training does not require a full instrument rating, the regulations mandate a minimum of 3 hours of instrument instruction, recognizing that flight inevitably encounters conditions in which visual references diminish or disappear entirely. Pilots must possess sufficient skill to navigate safely through these scenarios or, at a minimum, maintain aircraft control while executing emergency procedures.

The human vestibular system, that remarkable collection of fluid-filled canals within the inner ear that provides terrestrial balance and orientation, becomes a pilot's adversary once visual ground references vanish. Evolution perfected this biological gyroscope for creatures moving across the solid earth, where gravity's vector remains constant and visual confirmation continuously reinforces sensory input. The three-dimensional fluid environment of flight, however, introduces accelerations, decelerations, and banking forces that spectacularly confuse these sensory organs. A coordinated turn executed with perfect precision feels exactly like straight and level flight to a pilot without visual references, because the forces acting upon the body remain perpendicular to the aircraft's floor. Conversely, the sensation of banking often occurs when the plane flies perfectly straight, a phenomenon so convincing that pilots throughout aviation history have fought their instruments, sure that their body's signals indicated truth while gauges malfunctioned. The statistics are grimly instructive: non-instrument-rated pilots who continue flying into instrument meteorological conditions survive an average of just 178 seconds before losing aircraft control. This terrifying figure underscores why instrument instruction forms a mandatory component of private pilot training, even though the certificate's limitations explicitly prohibit intentional flight into clouds or conditions where visual references become inadequate.

The primary instrument panel transforms from a collection of circular gauges into a coherent story about the aircraft's relationship with three-dimensional space once pilots learn to scan systematically rather than fixate randomly. The attitude indicator, that gyroscopically stabilized representation of the artificial horizon, occupies the central position in standard instrument layouts because it conveys the most immediate information about pitch and bank. The miniature airplane silhouette remains fixed while the horizon line behind it tilts and moves, directly representing whether the aircraft climbs, descends, or banks left or right. Beginning students invariably stare at this single instrument, hypnotized by its immediate feedback, neglecting the other instruments that provide essential complementary information. The instructor's persistent reminder, "Scan, don't stare", becomes a mantra repeated throughout instrument training, teaching the systematic eye movement pattern that professional pilots employ unconsciously. This scan typically flows from attitude indicator to altimeter, confirming whether the aircraft maintains assigned altitude, then to airspeed indicator, verifying that velocity remains within appropriate ranges, then to heading indicator, ensuring that directional control continues, then to vertical speed indicator, checking rate of climb or descent, before returning to the attitude indicator as the scan's home base. The entire cycle takes perhaps two seconds, repeated continuously throughout flight, with each instrument contributing specific information while the overall pattern provides comprehensive awareness of the aircraft's state.

The distinction between control instruments and performance instruments separates novice instrument students from those developing genuine proficiency. The attitude indicator, power setting, and trim constitute the control instruments, the primary tools pilots use to command aircraft behavior. An altimeter, airspeed indicator, heading indicator, and vertical speed indicator serve as performance instruments, indicating whether the control inputs achieve the desired results. Students initially approach instrument flight as a reactive process, noticing that altitude has decreased by 50 feet and pulling back on the yoke to correct, only to discover 30 seconds later that altitude now exceeds the desired value by 75 feet, prompting a forward push that starts the cycle again. This oscillating chase around target parameters produces mental exhaustion and physical tension, the aircraft wandering through acceptable tolerances while the pilot works desperately harder. The breakthrough arrives when understanding shifts from reaction to precision establishment through proper attitude. A specific pitch attitude combined with a particular power setting produces predictable performance. Rather than chasing the altimeter's wandering needle, pilots learn to establish the attitude that generates level flight, then make minute adjustments based on performance instrument feedback, allowing the aircraft to stabilize into trim before assessing whether additional corrections prove necessary. This patience, this willingness to set conditions and wait for aircraft response rather than implementing continuous inputs, distinguishes smooth instrument flight from the herky-jerky corrections that characterize early training.

Instrument approaches to minimums —those procedures that guide aircraft through clouds down to mere hundreds of feet above ground before requiring visual contact with runways —remain beyond the scope of private pilot privileges and training. However, the fundamental skills supporting these precision approaches begin development during basic instrument instruction, establishing foundations that students may build upon should they pursue instrument ratings later. The localizer and glide slope, radio signals that provide horizontal and vertical guidance, respectively, appear on cockpit displays as simple crosshairs that pilots keep centered by adjusting heading and pitch. The initial experience feels analogous to balancing two separate seesaws simultaneously while riding a bicycle, each correction in one axis seemingly destabilizing the other. Intercepting the localizer from a forty-five-degree angle requires maintaining altitude perfectly while turning toward the inbound course, adjusting heading to compensate for crosswinds that drift the aircraft despite precise directional control. Rolling wings level precisely with the vertical needle centers. The glide slope intercept follows moments later, requiring power reduction and pitch adjustment that establishes a descent rate matching the signal's geometric slope, typically three degrees from horizontal. Student pilots discover that these procedures demand anticipation rather than reaction, with corrections implemented before deviations occur, and that they read instruments' trends and rates rather than their absolute positions. The workload intensity during these training exercises provides profound respect for instrument-rated pilots who execute these procedures in actual weather conditions, where missed approaches might require holds in crowded airspace. At the same time, fuel supplies dwindle and alternative airport options deteriorate.

Partial panel operations recreate scenarios where primary instruments fail, forcing pilots to navigate using backup systems that provide less intuitive information. The vacuum pump failure—a mechanical malfunction that simultaneously turns off both attitude and heading indicators—represents the most common and most serious instrument system emergency for light aircraft equipped with traditional instrumentation. When the instructor covers these instruments during training, simulating their failure, the remaining operational instruments —airspeed, altimeter, vertical speed indicator, magnetic compass, and turn coordinator —must provide sufficient information to maintain aircraft control and execute safe navigation. The turn coordinator, a small instrument typically relegated to peripheral awareness during normal operations, suddenly becomes crucial for maintaining wings-level flight and executing standard-rate turns. Its miniature airplane banks left or right, indicating turn direction and rate, while the slip-skid indicator below confirms coordination. The magnetic compass, that spinning card filled with mysterious oscillations and turning errors during normal operations, transforms into the primary directional reference despite its limitations. Students discover that flying a partial panel demands exceptional concentration, with the scan pattern adapting to gather attitude information from instrument combinations rather than from direct displays. Altitude changes detected on the vertical speed indicator, combined with airspeed trends, indicate whether pitch adjustment is required. A turn coordinator wings-level position, confirmed by stable altitude and airspeed, suggests successful straight flight despite the lack of a direct attitude reference. These exercises, though exhausting during training, provide essential skills for handling real emergencies where instrument failures occur without warning at precisely the wrong moments.

Unusual attitude recovery training introduces scenarios where pilots lose situational awareness completely, finding themselves in steep climbing turns or diving spirals without understanding how they arrived in these dangerous configurations. The procedure's name understates the terror many pilots experience when instructors simulate these situations, manipulating controls. At the same time, students close their eyes or look away, then suddenly announce, "You have the aircraft." Opening eyes to discover the attitude indicator showing a 60-degree bank and 20-degree nose-down pitch, airspeed rapidly increasing while the altimeter spins downward, triggers instinctive panic that training must override with disciplined recovery procedures. The rules for unusual attitude recovery seem almost counterintuitively simple: if the nose points low and airspeed increases, reduce power first, then level the wings, finally pull gently to raise the nose toward the horizon. The sequence matters critically because pulling while still banked tightens any spiral, increasing G-forces and worsening the situation, while reducing power before leveling wings keeps airspeed manageable throughout recovery. Unusual attitudes with the nose high, indicated by a decreasing airspeed and a climbing altimeter, require a different sequence: add power, lower the nose toward the horizon, level the wings, then adjust pitch for the desired flight parameters. These procedures, practiced repeatedly until they became reflexive rather than thoughtful, addressed the disorientation that claimed countless pilots before instrument training became standardized. The exercises also reveal how quickly aircraft attitudes can deteriorate once attention drifts from instrument scan, demonstrating why instrument flight demands such concentrated mental discipline.

The spatial disorientation demonstration is one of instrument training's most memorable and unsettling experiences, typically conducted when actual visual meteorological conditions exist. Still, the hood limits the student's vision to the instruments. The instructor directs the student to close their eyes completely, then executes a climbing turn in one direction, levels briefly, then descends in a turn toward the opposite direction, finally stabilizing in straight and level flight. After 30 seconds of this maneuvering, the instructor asks the student to describe the aircraft's current attitude solely based on vestibular sensation. The student's response, perhaps certain they're banking left and climbing, proves completely incorrect when eyes open to reveal straight-and-level flight confirmed by instruments. This demonstration, more than any lecture or textbook description, convinces students that subjective sensations are reliable during flight without visual references. The graveyard spiral, that insidious trap where pilots feel they're flying straight while actually descending in ever-tightening turns, becomes understandable after experiencing it firsthand. The pull of increased G-forces during the tightening spiral feels like climbing to pilots without instruments, prompting instinctive back-pressure on the yoke that steepens the bank and accelerates the descent. Breaking this illusion requires absolute faith in instruments contradicting every bodily sensation, a psychological challenge that explains why instrument flight training emphasizes trust over instinct.

Integration of navigation and communication tasks while maintaining precise instrument flight introduces workload management challenges that simulate realistic scenarios private pilots encounter during marginal weather conditions. The instructor assigns a heading to fly, an altitude to maintain, and an airspeed to achieve, then immediately begins asking questions about navigation frequencies, requiring students to reference approach plates or sectional charts while maintaining aircraft control. The heads-down time spent consulting charts causes altitude to drift, airspeed to vary, and heading to wander, quickly demonstrating why pilots require substantial practice before safely managing single-pilot instrument operations. The acronym aviate, navigate, communicate establishes a priority hierarchy that saves lives: first maintain aircraft control, second figure out where you're going, third talk to somebody about it. Students who reverse these priorities, attempting to answer ATC transmissions or locate navigation information while instruments show developing unusual attitudes, learn through immediate feedback why flying the airplane supersedes all other concerns. Professional pilots build the capacity for managing these concurrent demands through thousands of hours of experience. Still, private pilot students must recognize their limitations, understanding that accepting vectors from air traffic control or requesting delays for cockpit tasks demonstrates appropriate judgment rather than incompetence.

The relationship between instrument meteorological conditions and visual flight rules creates legal and practical boundaries that private pilots must respect absolutely. The regulations define specific weather minimums for VFR flight, typically requiring three statute miles of visibility and defined cloud clearances that vary by airspace classification. These minimums represent legal limits, not safety recommendations, and conservative pilots establish personal minimums substantially higher than regulatory floors. The temptation to continue VFR flight as weather gradually deteriorates proves seductive, each incremental reduction in visibility or lowering of the cloud deck seeming manageable until, suddenly, the cumulative effect creates genuine IMC that traps pilots without instrument ratings in clouds or reduced visibility, where spatial disorientation threatens imminent disaster. The instrument training component of private pilot certification provides escape capability, sufficient skill to execute a controlled one-hundred-eighty-degree turn back toward better conditions, and the ability to maintain aircraft control while receiving vectors from air traffic control toward an airport. This training does not authorize intentional flight into instrument conditions, and legal restrictions appropriately prohibit such operations without instrument rating certification. However, weather conditions change, forecast accuracy proves imperfect, and situations arise where inadvertent IMC encounters occur despite careful planning. The pilots who survive these scenarios consistently demonstrate characteristics established during instrument training: they immediately transition to instruments upon losing visual references, they communicate their situation to ATC rather than attempting to navigate independently, they avoid panic-driven maneuvering that leads to spatial disorientation, and they accept assistance rather than pretending competence they lack.

The psychological aspects of instrument flight challenge pilots differently than visual flight operations, creating mental fatigue that surprises students accustomed to hour-long visual practice sessions. The sustained concentration required for instrument scan, combined with the counterintuitive nature of trusting gauges over sensations, consumes cognitive resources at a rate that makes thirty-minute instrument sessions feel longer than two-hour visual cross-country flights. Students notice this fatigue manifesting as degraded scan discipline, fixation on single instruments, and delayed recognition of developing deviations from assigned parameters. The instructor's periodic callouts—"altitude," "heading," or "scan"—serve as cognitive resets, breaking fixation and restoring proper instrument monitoring. These interventions demonstrate why single-pilot instrument operations require extensive training before certification; the absence of a second set of eyes means pilots must maintain their own scan discipline without external prompting for extended flight durations that may exceed multiple hours. Developing this stamina requires practice that systematically extends instrument time while maintaining proficiency standards, gradually building capacity for sustained operations. Private pilot instrument training typically includes several sessions specifically designed to simulate scenarios in which basic instrument flight continues for extended periods, perhaps flying Victor airways between VORs while maintaining precise altitude and heading, preparing students for occasions when haze or poor visibility requires prolonged instrument reference despite remaining legally VFR.

The advancement from basic instrument skills practiced in benign visual meteorological conditions to more challenging scenarios simulating realistic weather encounters marks significant progress in pilot development. The instructor introduces distractions and complications that mirror actual operations: radio frequency changes at critical moments, unexpected turbulence simulated through control inputs, navigational errors requiring heading corrections, and traffic advisories demanding vigilance outside the cockpit despite primary attention remaining on instruments. These compound scenarios reveal how quickly task saturation develops when multiple demands compete simultaneously, demonstrating why accident reports frequently cite pilot overload as a contributing factor. The capacity to shed less critical tasks during high-workload periods develops through recognizing that perfection becomes impossible when circumstances exceed personal capabilities. A private pilot who encounters deteriorating weather while navigating toward an unfamiliar airport makes the correct decision by accepting air traffic control vectors rather than attempting independent navigation while maintaining instrument flight and managing radios. Similarly, abandoning attempts to reach the original destination and instead diverting toward nearby airports with better weather demonstrates sound judgment that keeps the hierarchy of priorities properly ordered. Instrument training sessions that deliberately overload students, pushing them beyond comfortable limits, teach these lessons in controlled environments where instructor intervention prevents actual danger while allowing students to experience the consequences of poor task prioritization.

The integration of instrument training throughout the private pilot certification process reflects regulatory recognition that the artificial separation between visual and instrument flight creates a false dichotomy that contradicts operational reality. Every flight involves instruments to some degree, whether monitoring altitude assignments in controlled airspace, maintaining cruise flight parameters during long cross-country flights, or simply verifying that performance matches pilot intentions. The systematic scan patterns developed during formal instrument training translate directly to visual operations, providing a structured approach to cockpit monitoring that prevents fixation and maintains comprehensive awareness. Pilots who properly internalize these scan techniques discover that their visual flying improves, situational awareness increases, and early detection of developing problems becomes habitual rather than a matter of luck. The attitude indicator remains useful even in severe clear weather, providing unambiguous information about bank angles during turn entries and recoveries. In contrast, the vertical speed indicator reveals subtle climb or descent trends before altimeter deviations become significant. This instrument integration represents evolved airmanship where tools work collectively to support decision-making rather than serving only as emergency backups when visual flight becomes impossible.

The transition from training to practical application occurs gradually as private pilots build experience managing various weather conditions within their certificated privileges. The instrument skills practiced under the hood during training become subconscious capabilities that are automatically accessed when haze reduces horizon definition or scattered clouds require brief encounters with instrument meteorological conditions during VFR climbs or descents. The pilot who maintains composure during these moments, seamlessly transitioning to instruments when visual references diminish, then back to visual flight when conditions improve, demonstrates the competence that instrument training sought to develop. These experiences build confidence appropriately, fostering realistic self-assessment of personal capabilities while maintaining healthy respect for situations beyond current skill levels. The private pilot who acknowledges limitations, requests lower altitudes to remain clear of clouds, or cancels flights when forecast conditions suggest marginal weather demonstrates maturity that instrument training helped develop through exposing students to the workload and concentration that actual instrument operations demand. This recognition that three hours of instrument training provides emergency capability rather than proficiency for sustained operations represents essential wisdom separating prudent aviators from those who mistake limited exposure for comprehensive competence.

The decision to pursue instrument rating certification after completing private pilot training appeals strongly to pilots who discovered during basic instrument instruction that this flying discipline's precision and procedural structure resonates with their personal inclinations. The complete instrument rating requires substantially more training — typically 40 hours of instrument flight, including complex approaches, holds, and airway navigation — that significantly exceeds the private pilot curriculum. However, the foundational skills established during private pilot instrument training —scan discipline, attitude flying, unusual attitude recovery, and navigation using instrumentation — provide the essential building blocks that advanced training develops into full proficiency. Many pilots report that instrument training, despite its challenging nature and intensive demands, provides the most professionally rewarding advancement in their aviation careers, transforming flying from fair-weather recreation into true transportation capability reliable across broader weather conditions. The precision required for instrument operations, the procedural discipline demanded by airway navigation, and the professionalism inherent in communicating within the instrument flight rules system create flying experiences qualitatively different from those of visual operations while building skills that enhance overall aviation competence.

The art of precision that instrument training introduces reaches far beyond the immediate goal of maintaining aircraft control without visual references, establishing habits and attitudes that characterize excellent pilots regardless of whether they operate under visual or instrument flight rules. The patience to set conditions and allow aircraft response rather than implementing constant corrections, the discipline to maintain systematic scan patterns rather than fixating on single information sources, the judgment to prioritize tasks appropriately when workload exceeds comfortable capacity, and the humility to request assistance rather than pretending independent competence all develop through instrument training experiences. These characteristics translate directly to every aspect of aviation, creating pilots who approach flying with methodical precision, who trust objective information over subjective impressions, and who recognize that safety depends upon established procedures followed consistently rather than improvisational responses to developing situations. The gauges on the instrument panel — those circular representations of complex aircraft systems and performance parameters — become a second language through which aircraft communicate with pilots willing to learn their grammar and syntax. Fluency in this language transforms instrument training from an uncomfortable requirement into essential education, providing capabilities that serve throughout aviation careers while establishing the foundation for adventures that span continents and weather conditions that would ground pilots lacking these precision skills. The hood may eventually be retired to storage compartments, as it is no longer needed as a training aid. Still, the lessons learned peering through its restricted vision remain permanent additions to pilot capabilities, ready for instant application whenever circumstances demand that dreams of flight continue regardless of whether visual references extend to horizons or terminate at windscreen edges obscured by clouds that make precision instrument flying the only path home.

The progression from basic instrument training to actual weather decision-making crystallizes during cross-country flights where forecast conditions and observed reality diverge in ways that test pilot judgment beyond simple stick-and-rudder skills. A flight planned for clear skies encounters unexpected haze layers that reduce visibility from the advertised 50 miles to perhaps 5, transforming distant landmarks from obvious waypoints into vague smudges barely distinguishable from terrain features. The pilot who confidently navigated previous cross-country flights by visual reference now finds that dead reckoning and radio navigation have become the primary techniques, with VOR needles and GPS tracks providing certainty that visual references cannot. This situation remains legally VFR, visibility exceeds regulatory minimums, and cloud clearances remain adequate, yet the psychological experience resembles instrument conditions sufficiently that pilots without solid instrument training often experience mounting anxiety that clouds judgment and decision-making. The instrument scan practiced during training sessions becomes a survival technique during these flights, providing structured cockpit activity that channels nervous energy into productive monitoring while confirming that aircraft performance remains stable despite reduced external references.

The distinction between mechanical instrument scanning and proper situational awareness represents an advancement that only develops through extensive practice combined with reflective analysis of what instruments actually reveal. Novice instrument students mechanically follow scan patterns, noting each instrument's indication without synthesizing the information into a comprehensive understanding of the aircraft's state and trajectory. The altimeter reads 3,500 feet, the airspeed shows 105 knots, and the heading indicates 270 degrees; these are separate facts lacking integration into a meaningful narrative. Experienced pilots perceive these same indications as a coherent story: aircraft maintaining cruise altitude in level flight, tracking westbound at normal cruise speed, suggesting proper power setting and trim configuration with no significant winds affecting performance. This gestalt perception develops gradually over hundreds of instrument scan cycles, in which individual readings coalesce into pattern recognition, much as individual letters eventually become words that convey meaning without conscious analysis of each character's shape.

Chapter 9: Facing Challenges: Overcoming Airborne Obstacles

The training progression toward private pilot certification follows a deliberately structured curriculum that builds competence through incremental mastery. Yet, no syllabus can fully anticipate the individual obstacles that transform straightforward lessons into personal crucibles. Every pilot's journey encounters unique challenges that resist the methodical approach that has worked successfully for other aspects of training. These stumbling blocks arrive without warning, a maneuver that refuses to click despite dozens of attempts, weather patterns that consistently force cancellations during critical training phases, or equipment failures that erode confidence just when momentum builds toward checkride readiness. The ability to recognize, confront, and overcome these airborne obstacles separates those who eventually earn their wings from those whose logbooks gather dust, training incomplete. Understanding that challenges are a regular part of the learning process rather than personal failures provides the psychological foundation for persistence when progress stalls and frustration threatens to overwhelm determination.

Physical coordination difficulties may present the most humbling obstacle for students whose professional accomplishments in other domains set expectations for rapid mastery. The physician who performs delicate surgical procedures discovers that hands accustomed to precise instrument manipulation somehow produce jerky, over-controlled inputs on the yoke. The software engineer whose logical mind effortlessly navigates complex code finds the simultaneous management of throttle, mixture, and propeller controls overwhelmingly confusing. These coordination challenges stem from the unique requirement for aviation to integrate multiple simultaneous inputs across different control axes while processing visual information, monitoring instruments, communicating on radio frequencies, and maintaining situational awareness. The human brain naturally excels at sequential task completion but initially struggles with the parallel-processing demands of flight, particularly when spatial orientation challenges inherent to three-dimensional maneuvering are added. Students encountering these physical coordination barriers often experience profound frustration because the difficulty feels insurmountable; the mind understands what needs to be accomplished, but the body refuses to comply with sufficient precision. Breaking through this barrier requires accepting that coordination develops through repetition and muscle memory rather than intellectual understanding, that the hundreds of minor corrections and adjustments eventually become subconscious responses requiring no deliberate thought, much as experienced automobile drivers change gears or adjust speed without conscious attention to the mechanical processes involved.

The plateau phenomenon strikes unpredictably, often appearing after periods of excellent progress when competence seems nearly achieved. Students who advanced confidently through early lessons suddenly find themselves unable to execute maneuvers that felt polished just days earlier. Landings that consistently greased onto the centerline with satisfying chirps now balloon, drop hard, or drift left despite apparently identical approach parameters. Radio communications that flowed smoothly during recent flights now emerge as stammering fragments requiring multiple transmissions to convey simple requests. These plateaus create deep discouragement because regression defies logical expectations; skills should improve or stabilize, not mysteriously deteriorate without apparent cause. The psychological impact intensifies when instructors seem unable to identify specific errors, offer only encouraging platitudes about persistence, and suggest more practice as a solution. Yet aviation educators recognize plateaus as neurological phenomena occurring during complex skill acquisition, representing periods when the brain consolidates previously learned information and reorganizes neural pathways to accommodate increasingly sophisticated performance levels. The conscious incompetence that marks plateau periods actually signals that learning continues at subconscious levels. However, external performance temporarily degrades while internal processing reorganizes accumulated knowledge into more efficient operational frameworks. Students who understand this mechanism can reframe plateaus from evidence of failure into confirmation that learning progresses toward higher competence levels. However, patience and continued practice remain essential for breakthrough moments that inevitably follow sustained effort.

Financial pressures create obstacles distinct from technical challenges but equally capable of derailing training completion. The initial estimates provided by flight schools are often optimistic, based on assumptions of consistent weather, rapid student progress, and minimal lesson repetition. Reality introduces unexpected expenses, extra hours needed to master challenging maneuvers, aircraft maintenance delays requiring rental of more expensive alternatives, checkride discontinuities necessitating additional examiner fees, and medical certificate renewals with specialist consultations for previously unknown conditions. Students who budget precisely for the minimum required hours often find themselves halfway through training with depleted resources and certification still distant. The financial stress compounds when training interruptions become necessary to rebuild savings, introducing the additional problem of skill degradation during extended breaks from flying. Each month away from the cockpit erodes proficiency, requiring expensive refresher training before continuing toward new objectives, sometimes creating cycles where students repeatedly relearn previously mastered material without advancing toward certification. The most effective strategy for managing financial obstacles involves realistic budgeting that adds substantial contingency beyond minimum requirements, recognizing that most students require fifteen to twenty percent more flight hours than regulatory minimums before achieving consistent performance warranting checkride scheduling. Additionally, maintaining open communication with instructors about financial constraints enables creative solutions, such as focusing on ground instruction during resource limitations, using flight simulation for procedure practice, or scheduling intensive training blocks when funds accumulate rather than spreading lessons thinly across months with insufficient frequency for skill retention.

Psychological barriers often prove more challenging than physical or financial obstacles because they resist straightforward solutions and sometimes remain invisible even to students experiencing them. Fear represents the most obvious psychological challenge, though its manifestations vary dramatically across individuals. Some students experience generalized anxiety about aviation safety; their imaginations populate every flight with catastrophic scenarios, despite statistical evidence demonstrating general aviation's reasonable safety record when conducted appropriately. Others develop specific phobias following uncomfortable experiences; persistent turbulence during an early lesson creates enduring anxiety whenever winds gust, or a rough landing generates ongoing tension during every approach. The most insidious fear arises gradually as knowledge deepens and students become aware of the myriad ways aviation can punish inattention or poor judgment, transforming innocent confidence into a paralysis-inducing hyper-vigilance that prevents the relaxed flying necessary for smooth aircraft control. Beyond fear, perfectionism creates psychological obstacles that seem positive traits but actually impede learning by establishing impossible standards where anything short of flawless performance represents failure. Perfectionistic students become frustrated by standard learning curves, interpreting each mistake as evidence of inadequacy rather than recognizing errors as essential feedback mechanisms enabling improvement. This mindset creates tension that degrades performance, establishing self-reinforcing cycles in which anxiety about making mistakes produces the very errors feared, confirming internal narratives of incompetence despite objective evidence of satisfactory progress.

Interpersonal conflicts with instructors occasionally create obstacles that require difficult navigation, as effective learning depends on productive working relationships built on mutual respect and clear communication. Personality mismatches occur despite both parties' best intentions. The methodical instructor who provides detailed explanations frustrates the kinesthetic learner who prefers hands-on experimentation. In contrast, the casual instructor who adopts a friendly, informal style frustrates the structured student seeking systematic progression through clearly defined objectives. Sometimes conflicts arise from genuine instructional deficiencies rather than simple personality differences, particularly at schools with high instructor turnover where newly minted commercial pilots build hours before moving to airline positions. These inexperienced instructors may lack the pedagogical sophistication to adapt teaching styles to individual learning preferences or may demonstrate insufficient knowledge of subjects beyond their immediate experience. Students face difficult decisions when instructor relationships deteriorate because aviation culture emphasizes loyalty and gratitude toward instructors while simultaneously recognizing that productive learning requires effective teaching. The emotional complexity intensifies when students genuinely like their instructors personally but realize that learning has stalled due to instructional limitations. Addressing these situations requires uncomfortable conversations in which students must advocate for their educational needs while maintaining professional courtesy, potentially requesting a change in instructor or seeking supplemental instruction from alternative sources. Flight schools generally accommodate such requests because they understand that compatible student-instructor pairings significantly impact training completion rates. Yet, students often delay these conversations due to misplaced guilt about seeming disloyal or demanding.

Medical certification obstacles arise unexpectedly during routine examinations when Aviation Medical Examiners discover conditions disqualifying applicants from pilot privileges or requiring special issuance authorizations that involve extensive documentation and FAA review. The seemingly simple physical examination that most students anticipate completing in thirty minutes occasionally reveals previously undiagnosed diabetes, evidence of past mental health treatment, cardiac abnormalities requiring specialist evaluation, or medication use incompatible with flight operations. These discoveries transform straightforward training progression into prolonged waits while gathering medical records, obtaining specialist clearances, and navigating the Federal Aviation Administration's medical certification bureaucracy. Students sometimes learn that childhood diagnoses casually mentioned to AMEs, attention deficit disorders treated years ago, brief counseling following family trauma, or experimentation with medications during college, trigger extensive documentation requirements despite these conditions having no current impact on functioning. The uncertainty during medical certification delays creates profound stress because students cannot continue training toward solo flight or checkrides without valid medical certificates. Yet, the bureaucratic timeline remains unpredictable and largely beyond their control. Some conditions prove permanently disqualifying, forcing painful decisions about whether to abandon pilot ambitions or pursue sport pilot certification under driver's license medical standards with operational limitations. Others eventually achieve special issuance authorizations, but only after months of documentation, specialist visits, and FAA correspondence that drains both financial resources and emotional reserves. Students facing medical certification challenges benefit from consulting aviation medical specialists who understand the intricate requirements and can guide documentation strategies.

However, these consultations add to training budgets already strained by mounting costs.

Equipment reliability issues introduce obstacles ranging from minor annoyances to significant training disruptions that affect both schedule and psychology. Modern aircraft generally offer excellent reliability, yet the aging training fleets at many flight schools include aircraft with chronic maintenance issues that repeatedly ground planes just as students schedule essential lessons. The frustration compounds when maintenance delays repeatedly affect the same aircraft students have come to know intimately, forcing transitions to unfamiliar planes with different panel layouts, performance characteristics, and operational quirks that require adaptation time. More seriously, in-flight equipment failures, partial power losses, electrical system malfunctions, instrument failures, or landing gear complications create intense stress even when instructors manage situations safely. Students who experience these events sometimes develop persistent anxiety about aircraft reliability, conducting excessively detailed preflight inspections seeking assurance against failures that proper maintenance should prevent but cannot eliminate. The psychological impact extends beyond the immediate incident when students replay scenarios, wondering what might have happened during solo flight without instructor intervention and questioning whether their decision-making would have ensured equally positive outcomes. Processing these experiences requires honest debriefing, where instructors acknowledge legitimate concerns while providing context on system redundancies, emergency procedures, and the remarkable reliability records that modern aircraft achieve despite occasional component failures. Students need permission to feel unsettled by equipment problems rather than having concerns dismissed with cavalier assertions that "these things happen," while simultaneously receiving guidance about appropriate precautions versus counterproductive hypervigilance that transforms flying from an enjoyable challenge into an anxiety-producing ordeal.

Weather-related training interruptions create cascading obstacles that go beyond mere scheduling inconvenience, particularly for students balancing flight training with demanding work and family obligations. The carefully arranged lesson, scheduled months in advance during a narrow window of availability, gets cancelled three hours beforehand when morning fog fails to lift as forecast or when afternoon thunderstorms develop earlier than predicted. The next available slot may not appear for weeks, causing the skill degradation problems mentioned earlier and disrupting the training momentum essential for efficient progression. Students in regions with challenging weather patterns, coastal areas with frequent marine layers, mountain locations with afternoon convection, or northern climates with extended winter weather limitations face pronounced challenges maintaining consistent training frequency. The frustration intensifies when students observe commercial traffic operating normally while training flights remain grounded due to more conservative weather minimums appropriate for student operations. This discrepancy sometimes puts pressure on instructors to bend minimums slightly, creating unsafe dynamics in which students advocate for marginal weather flights that instructors must refuse, despite disappointing students eager to progress. Managing weather interruptions effectively requires realistic expectations about seasonal patterns that affect training duration, as well as the flexibility to capitalize on favorable conditions when they arrive, even if that means rearranging other commitments to accommodate unexpected weather windows. Students who establish clear communication with instructors about availability can receive short-notice schedule adjustments when improving weather creates opportunities. However, this flexibility demands lifestyle arrangements that may not be compatible with rigid work schedules or family responsibilities.

Explicit performance anxiety related to checkride preparation represents a distinct obstacle that emerges late in training, as students transition from learning mode to evaluation preparation. The skills demonstrated consistently during routine lessons somehow deteriorate when students consciously think "this is checkride preparation" or when conducting mock checkrides with chief instructors serving as examiner proxies. The phenomenon mirrors test anxiety that students may have experienced during academic examinations, though aviation's practical nature and safety implications intensify the pressure considerably. Students who performed complex cross-country flights competently suddenly struggle with basic pilotage during checkride preparation, not due to knowledge deficits but because anxiety interferes with information processing and decision-making. Radio communications become stilted and error-prone under the imagined scrutiny of evaluation, even though they flowed naturally during previous flights. Maneuvers executed to tight standards during practice deteriorate to barely acceptable levels when students mentally rehearse examiner critiques rather than focusing on immediate flying tasks. This performance anxiety sometimes leads to false starts, with students scheduling checkrides before they are genuinely ready, because instructors and chief pilots issue endorsements based on demonstrated capability. Yet, the students cancel or discontinue examinations when anxiety prevents performance matching their actual skill levels. Breaking through this barrier requires exposure therapy, where students gradually acclimate to evaluation pressure through progressive mock checkrides and deliberate practice. At the same time, observers scrutinize techniques and cognitive strategies for managing intrusive thoughts about evaluation outcomes. Some students benefit from sports psychology techniques used by competitive athletes, including visualization exercises, imagining successful checkride completion, breathing techniques to manage physiological anxiety responses, and mental scripts that redirect attention from evaluation concerns to immediate task execution.

The challenge of competing priorities emerges when life circumstances complicate the single-minded focus optimal for efficient training completion. Family obligations, career demands, financial pressures, health issues, and relationship dynamics all compete for the attention and resources required for flight training. Students who begin training during stable life periods sometimes encounter unexpected complications, job changes requiring relocation mid-training, family health crises demanding caregiving, relationship difficulties that consume the emotional energy needed for learning complex skills, or financial reversals that force a suspension of training. These competing priorities create guilt regardless of the choices made and the continued training. At the same time, family situations demand attention, prompting remorse over misplaced priorities, while pausing training to address life complications can lead to frustration over delayed dream fulfillment. The challenge intensifies because aviation skills degrade during interruptions, meaning that eventually resuming training requires expensive refresher work before continuing toward certification. Students struggling with competing priorities benefit from honest conversations with family members about the importance of training and the resources necessary, seeking their genuine support rather than proceeding despite their reluctance or resentment. Sometimes the wise decision is to temporarily pause training until life circumstances stabilize, rather than forcing on with training that strains relationships and produces suboptimal learning due to divided attention. Aviation opportunities remain available indefinitely, and training completed during stable, supportive life periods proves more efficient and enjoyable than efforts forced during chaotic circumstances where flying becomes an additional stressor rather than fulfilling an aspiration.

Communication barriers occasionally arise from the technical nature of aviation instruction and the rapid pace at which complex information gets conveyed, particularly for students without mechanical or technical backgrounds. Instructors steeped in aviation culture sometimes forget that terminology, concepts, and procedures they consider fundamental remain entirely foreign to newcomers encountering this specialized knowledge domain. The resulting communication gaps leave students nodding along while inwardly confused, hesitant to admit incomprehension for fear of appearing slow or unintelligent. These gaps accumulate like compound interest; misunderstanding foundational concepts creates cascading confusion as subsequent lessons build upon knowledge never truly grasped. The problem intensifies when students come from high-achievement backgrounds where admitting confusion feels incompatible with self-image as capable learners who quickly master new domains. Additionally, some students struggle with learning styles poorly matched to standard instructional approaches, and visual learners founder when instructors rely primarily on verbal explanations. In contrast, kinesthetic learners need hands-on practice before theoretical discussions make sense. Breaking through communication barriers requires students to develop the confidence to explicitly request clarification, alternative explanations, or different instructional approaches without interpreting these requests as personal shortcomings. Effective instructors create psychological safety, where questions elicit enthusiastic responses rather than impatient sighs, recognizing that confusion signals engagement with the material rather than inattention or limited ability. Students can facilitate better communication by providing instructors with feedback on which explanations proved helpful and which remain unclear, enabling instructors to adjust their approaches to more effective teaching methods matched to individual learning preferences.

The final obstacle confronting many students is overcoming the internal voice that questions whether certification achievement justifies the substantial investment of time, money, and emotional energy required. This doubt arrives during challenging moments when progress stalls, costs exceed budgets, frustrations mount, and initial enthusiasm fades into grinding perseverance. The voice asks pointed questions difficult to dismiss. Wouldn't these resources serve better purposes, such as home improvements, children's education, or retirement savings? Does recreational flying really merit this level of commitment when family members barely tolerate the time diverted from shared activities? Will aviation actually deliver the satisfaction imagined during initial inspiration, or will the reality prove disappointing once the novelty fades? These doubts carry particular weight because they contain legitimate elements, flying does cost substantially more than many recreational activities, and post-certification flying requires ongoing expenses for aircraft rental, currency maintenance, and insurance that challenge many household budgets. Addressing these doubts requires returning to the fundamental motivations that initiated training and honestly evaluating whether those motivations remain valid or have evolved as training has provided a clearer understanding of aviation realities. Some students discover that their initial dream of flight stemmed from romantic notions about aviation freedom that don't align with the experience of regulatory compliance, careful planning, and conservative risk management that characterize responsible flying. Others confirm that aviation fulfills deep yearnings for challenge, competence development, and experiences transcending ordinary life that justify the investments required. The decision to persist or pause involves no universal answer; some individuals wisely recognize that continuing training serves ego rather than genuine passion, while others find renewed commitment by reconnecting with the profound satisfaction that drew them skyward initially.

Overcoming these diverse airborne obstacles requires cultivating resilience —the psychological capacity to persist through difficulties while maintaining emotional equilibrium and forward progress. Resilient students reframe setbacks as temporary challenges that require problem-solving rather than as permanent failures signaling inadequacy. They develop tolerance for discomfort, recognizing that learning necessarily involves periods of confusion, frustration, and performance below desired standards. They seek support from multiple sources —instructors, fellow students, online aviation communities, and non-aviation friends and family — who provide perspective when aviation challenges feel overwhelming. Most importantly, resilient students maintain a connection to the fundamental joy of flight that transcends obstacles, finding moments — even in challenging lessons — when the profound privilege of commanding an aircraft through three-dimensional space overrides temporary frustrations with learning. These students develop the emotional maturity to acknowledge difficulties honestly while refusing to let challenges define their entire training experience; instead, they view obstacles as plot complications in longer narratives, ultimately culminating in successful certification and the beginning of lifelong aviation adventures that justify the struggles required to achieve that milestone.

The recognition that obstacles represent universal experiences rather than individual failings provides a crucial perspective during difficult training periods. Every certificated pilot navigated similar challenges, though the specific manifestations differed according to personal circumstances and learning profiles. The confident airline captain now commanding widebody aircraft across oceans struggled with radio communications during primary training, freezing during initial calls to busy tower controllers and requiring dozens of practice sessions before transmissions flowed naturally. The accomplished aerobatic performer, whose graceful routines captivate airshow audiences, spent frustrating months battling airsickness during early training, wondering whether constitutional incompatibility with aviation would force abandoning pilot aspirations despite a passionate desire to fly.

The flight instructor who now guides students through their own challenges with patient expertise once sat in the same seat experiencing identical doubts, frustrations, and moments of despair when certification seemed impossibly distant.

Understanding this universality helps students resist the cognitive distortion that their particular struggles indicate unique inadequacy while everyone else progresses smoothly toward inevitable success. Social comparison becomes particularly toxic in aviation training environments, where students naturally observe peers who seem to advance effortlessly, their apparent mastery creating unfavorable contrasts with their own personal difficulties. What remains invisible in these comparisons is the private struggles that seemingly successful students face in areas outside their own. The student who solos weeks earlier might be wrestling with cross-country planning anxiety not yet encountered, while the peer who executes beautiful landings consistently may be failing written examination practice tests repeatedly due to knowledge retention difficulties. Flight schools inadvertently compound comparison problems by celebrating milestone achievements, solo flights, checkride completions, and new ratings without acknowledging the obstacles overcome to reach those accomplishments, creating the impression of linear progression that doesn't reflect the messy reality of actual learning trajectories.

Developing a growth mindset — the psychological orientation that views abilities as developable through effort rather than fixed traits — provides robust protection against discouragement induced by obstacles. Students with growth mindsets interpret difficulties as information about where additional practice or alternative approaches might help rather than as verdicts about immutable limitations. When landings deteriorate during plateau periods, growth-oriented students ask, "What specific aspects need adjustment?" rather than concluding, "I'm not talented enough for this." This orientation transforms obstacles from threatening judgments into neutral challenges requiring problem-solving, fundamentally changing emotional responses to difficulties. The mindset shift doesn't eliminate frustration; struggling with challenging material remains uncomfortable regardless of interpretation—but it prevents it from metastasizing into a broader sense of self-doubt that undermines motivation and persistence. Students can deliberately cultivate growth mindsets by paying conscious attention to their internal dialogue, noticing and revising fixed-mindset statements like "I can't do this" into growth-oriented alternatives like "I haven't mastered this yet, but I'm improving with practice."

The role of self-compassion in overcoming obstacles deserves emphasis because aviation culture has historically embraced machismo attitudes that dismissed struggles as weakness to be overcome with greater determination. This outdated perspective ignored psychological research demonstrating that self-compassion, treating oneself with the same kindness one would extend to a struggling friend, actually enhances performance by reducing debilitating anxiety and shame that interfere with learning. Students who berate themselves for mistakes or difficulties activate stress responses that impair the cognitive flexibility and creative problem-solving needed for breakthrough moments. Conversely, students who acknowledge struggles with gentle understanding maintain the emotional resources necessary for continued effort and receptivity to feedback. Self-compassion doesn't mean lowering standards or accepting mediocre performance; instead, it involves maintaining high expectations while offering oneself patience and encouragement during the inevitable difficulties that accompany complex skill acquisition. The internal dialogue shifts from harsh criticism —"I screwed up that approach again, I'm such an idiot" —to constructive acknowledgment —"That approach didn't meet standards, let me think about what adjustments might help next time."

Ultimately, the obstacles encountered during flight training serve purposes beyond merely testing persistence. They develop judgment, resilience, and self-knowledge that prove invaluable throughout aviation careers. The student who navigates financial constraints by creatively maximizing limited resources develops the practical wisdom useful when weather diversions or unexpected maintenance create budget challenges during post-certification flying. The student who overcomes fear through gradual exposure and cognitive management builds emotional regulation skills essential for managing the inevitable anxious moments every pilot encounters when weather deteriorates unexpectedly or unfamiliar situations arise. The obstacles that seem unnecessarily complex during training actually prepare pilots for the reality that aviation consistently presents challenges that require calm problem-solving under pressure. The certification journey provides relatively safe opportunities to develop these capabilities with instructor support before confronting them alone.

Chapter 10: Preparing for the Checkride: Polishing Skills

The transition from training toward certification brings a subtle but profound shift in perspective that permeates every aspect of preparation during those final weeks before the practical test. Flight lessons no longer focus on introducing new concepts or building foundational skills; those elements have been established through months of instruction, practice, and refinement. Instead, training enters a polishing phase in which the rough edges of competence are smoothed into the smooth confidence expected of certificated pilots. This period demands a different mindset than earlier training phases, requiring students to view their flying through the critical lens of an examiner while simultaneously maintaining the relaxed proficiency that comes from genuine mastery rather than rote memorization. The checkride looms as both destination and gateway, representing completion of one journey and commencement of another, and these final preparation weeks determine whether candidates approach that threshold with justified confidence or lingering doubts that undermine performance during the most scrutinized flight of their training career.

The Federal Aviation Administration's Airman Certification Standards document becomes a constant companion during this preparation period, its pages worn from repeated review as students dissect each task's objective, required knowledge, and acceptable performance parameters. Unlike earlier training phases, where instructors selected lesson content and practice sequences, checkride preparation demands that students take ownership of their readiness assessment, identifying specific weak areas requiring additional practice while maintaining proficiency in tasks already mastered. This self-directed learning represents a maturation process where spoon-fed instruction gives way to personal responsibility for skill maintenance and improvement. The ACS contains no surprises; every maneuver, every knowledge area, every procedure tested during the practical exam appears explicitly within its pages, organized by area of operation and task. Yet despite this complete transparency, candidates routinely discover gaps in their preparation when reviewing the document systematically, finding specific elements they can perform adequately, but not to the precision standards the examiner will expect. Perhaps slow flight becomes ragged below best angle-of-climb speed, or pilotage navigation lacks the systematic checkpoint identification demonstrating thorough flight planning, or radio communications become hurried and unprofessional under stress. These discoveries, uncomfortable though they may be, provide invaluable opportunities for targeted improvement before facing evaluation rather than discovering deficiencies during the checkride when correction becomes impossible.

The concept of acceptable performance standards deserves careful consideration during this polishing phase, as many students mistakenly believe checkride success requires perfect execution throughout every maneuver and task. This perfectionist mindset creates unnecessary pressure and can degrade performance by introducing tension that disrupts the smooth, relaxed control inputs characteristic of proficient flying. The ACS explicitly defines tolerance ranges for altitude, heading, airspeed, and other parameters, recognizing that aviation involves managing dynamic forces constantly requiring correction rather than achieving static perfection. A steep turn performed within 100 feet of entry altitude throughout the maneuver meets certification standards in full. Yet, many candidates torture themselves when the altitude deviates by 50 feet, treating normal performance variation as catastrophic failure. Understanding the difference between meaningful errors requiring correction and minor deviations within acceptable tolerances allows candidates to maintain composure during evaluation, correcting smoothly when necessary without panicking over inconsequential variations that examiners dismiss as normal flying. This calibrated self-assessment requires practice, as student pilots typically lack sufficient experience to judge whether performance meets standards without instructor validation. Mock checkrides conducted by different instructors provide invaluable calibration opportunities, exposing candidates to various evaluator styles while receiving expert assessment of whether their flying genuinely meets certification standards or requires further refinement.

Chairflying emerges as an essential preparation technique during these final weeks, allowing students to mentally rehearse procedures, maneuvers, and decision sequences without aircraft rental costs or weather delays. The term "chairflying" understates the technique's sophistication; effective practice involves far more than passively imagining flight sequences while sitting comfortably. Serious chairflying requires creating a realistic environment — perhaps sitting in an actual cockpit or replicating the seating position and hand placements used during flight — then methodically working through procedures with precise detail, including every switch position, verbal callouts, instrument scan patterns, and control inputs. Champions of every domain employ mental rehearsal to reinforce correct sequences and build automated responses that emerge smoothly during actual performance, and pilots benefit equally from this proven training methodology. The checkride contains numerous procedures where mental rehearsal proves especially valuable: the pre-takeoff briefing covering emergency procedures and abort criteria; the GUMPS check before landing, ensuring gear-down-welded confirmation and fuel selector position; the go-around decision process when landing becomes unstable; and the lost procedures sequence when pilotage navigation encounters unexpected confusion. Each procedure becomes smoother and more automatic through repeated mental rehearsal, building neural pathways that activate correctly under examination stress when conscious thought processes may become compromised by adrenaline and pressure.

Aircraft systems knowledge requires particular attention during checkride preparation because oral examination questions probe not merely surface understanding but genuine comprehension of how components interact and why specific design choices were made. Earlier training phases introduced systems gradually, often accepting functional understanding without demanding detailed mechanical knowledge. A student learning basic maneuvers needs to understand that mixture controls fuel-air ratio without necessarily comprehending venturi principles or fuel metering mechanisms. As checkride preparation intensifies, however, this superficial understanding becomes insufficient. Examiners probe deeper, asking about alternative air sources when carburetor ice occurs, electrical load priorities when alternator failure requires battery conservation, and the specific conditions that promote vapor lock in fuel systems. These questions assess whether candidates possess the systems knowledge necessary to troubleshoot malfunctions and make informed decisions when abnormal situations arise during flight. The aircraft's Pilot Operating Handbook becomes required reading during this preparation phase, its systems section deserving the same careful study previously devoted to performance charts and limitations. Many students discover they have been flying for months without truly understanding how the vacuum system powers gyroscopic instruments, or why magneto checks detect internal coil deterioration, or what actually happens when selecting carburetor heat beyond "it prevents ice." This deeper systems understanding transforms pilots from aircraft operators into aircraft managers capable of diagnosing problems and implementing appropriate solutions rather than simply following memorized procedures without comprehension.

Weight and balance calculations receive renewed emphasis during checkride preparation, as examiners frequently test this critical knowledge area through scenarios requiring detailed computation and analysis. The mathematics involved remains relatively simple: multiplication, addition, and division that any high school graduate can perform, yet many candidates struggle with weight-and-balance problems because they focus on computational mechanics rather than understanding the underlying concepts that explain why aircraft behavior changes with different loading configurations. An aircraft loaded within weight limits but with the center of gravity aft of the acceptable range becomes dangerously unstable in pitch, requiring constant forward control pressure and exhibiting potential for unrecoverable stalls. Conversely, forward center of gravity loading increases stability but degrades climb performance and extends landing distances because greater tail-down force is required for pitch control. These practical implications matter far more than merely generating correct numbers on loading forms. Yet, checkride preparation often emphasizes computational accuracy while neglecting the conceptual understanding that transforms calculations into meaningful safety decisions. Adequate preparation involves working through multiple weight-and-balance scenarios with different passenger and baggage configurations, fuel loads, and mission profiles, analyzing not just whether each configuration falls within acceptable envelopes but also how the different loadings affect aircraft performance and handling characteristics. This analytical approach develops intuition about loading effects, allowing pilots to recognize problematic configurations immediately rather than requiring detailed calculations to detect dangerous situations.

Emergency procedures represent another critical preparation area deserving of systematic review and practice during the weeks leading up to the checkride. Earlier training phases introduced emergency responses incrementally, typically beginning with engine failures during pattern work, where troubleshooting time remains minimal and landing areas appear prominent. As training progressed, emergency scenarios became more complex, failures at higher altitudes allowed troubleshooting attempts, off-field landings in challenging terrain, electrical failures at night, and partial power losses requiring diversion decisions. By the time of checkride preparation, students should have experienced the full range of emergency scenarios they might encounter during practical testing. Yet many discover that their emergency responses have become stale due to a lack of recent practice. Instructors understandably focus final training sessions on polishing standard procedures and refining maneuvers rather than practicing emergency responses, creating a dangerous readiness gap if candidates neglect emergency procedure review during independent preparation. The emergency procedures checklist must become so familiar that each item comes to mind without conscious recall, allowing pilots to initiate appropriate responses immediately while confirming actions against printed procedures. This depth of familiarity emerges only through repeated practice and systematic review, mentally rehearsing emergency sequences until they become automatic responses emerging smoothly under stress. The examiner expects not merely correct procedural responses but calm, methodical execution demonstrating that the candidate's emergency training has developed genuine competence rather than superficial memorization.

Scenario-based training becomes increasingly important during checkride preparation as instructors shift from isolated maneuver practice to integrated flight experiences that reflect realistic mission profiles. A typical checkride includes cross-country planning and navigation, various maneuvers in the practice area, simulated emergency procedures, and pattern work, including go-arounds and different landing configurations, all integrated into a complete flight experience rather than disconnected tasks. Preparation should mirror this integrated structure, with training flights incorporating multiple elements into coherent scenarios rather than focusing exclusively on individual maneuvers. Perhaps a preparation flight begins with a cross-country departure toward a planned destination, then diverts to the practice area for maneuvers when the instructor introduces weather deterioration at the original destination, completes required maneuvers, including emergency procedures and pilotage navigation toward an alternate airport, then returns for landing practice at the home field, including full-stop landings and simulated go-arounds. This scenario-based approach develops the task management and prioritization skills necessary during checkride evaluation when multiple demands compete for attention simultaneously. Students accustomed to focusing exclusively on single tasks often struggle during practical tests when examiners introduce complications, such as requesting frequency changes during approach or asking systems questions. At the same time, the candidate navigates realistic multitasking situations that require workload management skills developed through scenario-based training.

Aeronautical decision-making deserves explicit attention during checkride preparation, as examiners evaluate not just technical flying skills but also judgment and risk-management abilities that distinguish safe pilots from those who contribute to accident statistics. The FAA's risk management emphasis has intensified in recent years, with the Airman Certification Standards requiring explicit demonstration of hazard identification and risk mitigation throughout the practical test. This emphasis reflects accident data showing that most aviation incidents result from poor decision-making rather than inadequate stick-and-rudder skills, pilots flying VFR into instrument conditions, attempting operations beyond their capabilities, or continuing flights despite accumulating warning signs that prudent judgment would recognize as requiring changed plans. Checkride preparation must therefore include systematic analysis of decision points throughout flight operations, identifying where hazards exist and what mitigation strategies apply. The decision to fly or cancel on checkride day itself is a critical judgment point, as marginal weather can pressure pilots to launch even when conditions exceed personal minimums or regulatory requirements. Candidates must demonstrate willingness to postpone evaluation rather than accepting unnecessary risks, showing examiners that safety priorities genuinely supersede schedule convenience. This judgment extends throughout the checkride experience, recognizing when practice-area traffic density requires moving to a different location for maneuver practice, initiating go-arounds when landings become unstable rather than forcing a touchdown, and choosing conservative interpretations when cloud-clearance requirements become ambiguous. These judgment demonstrations convince examiners that candidates possess the mature decision-making skills necessary to operate safely without instructor supervision.

Performance planning is subjected to detailed scrutiny during practical tests, requiring candidates to demonstrate a thorough understanding of how atmospheric conditions, aircraft weight, and runway characteristics affect takeoff and landing distances, climb performance, and cruise speeds. Many students approach performance planning superficially, selecting cruise altitudes based on convenience rather than systematically analyzing the effects of wind and temperature at different altitudes, or failing to consider density altitude when operating from high-elevation airports on warm days. Checkride preparation should include detailed performance analysis for the planned test flight, calculating actual takeoff and landing distances based on forecast conditions rather than assuming standard performance, determining the optimum cruise altitude based on winds aloft and terrain clearance requirements, and identifying any performance limitations given the planned aircraft loading. This detailed planning demonstrates professional-level preparation while building familiarity with performance chart usage that many candidates find intimidating due to complex interpolation requirements and multiple variables affecting calculations. Examiners frequently present performance scenarios during oral examination. What happens to the takeoff distance when the temperature increases by thirty degrees? How does the climb rate change with altitude increases? What factors determine whether an obstacle clearance situation requires aborting takeoff? These questions assess whether candidates genuinely understand performance principles rather than merely following cookbook procedures. The best preparation involves working multiple performance problems with varying conditions, developing intuition about how atmospheric changes affect aircraft capabilities, rather than requiring detailed calculations for every assessment.

Communication skills deserve focused attention during final preparation, as many checkride candidates exhibit radio communication proficiencies that work adequately during training flights but reveal weaknesses under examination pressure. Radio work seems deceptively simple after months of training flights. Yet many students develop bad habits their instructors tolerate — such as incomplete position reports, improper phraseology, and hesitant transmissions that reveal uncertainty. These communication shortcuts become problematic during checkride evaluation when examiners assess whether candidates communicate with the professionalism expected of certificated pilots. Effective radio communication requires planning before transmitting, organizing information logically in accordance with standard formats, speaking clearly at an appropriate speed, and listening carefully to understand controller instructions and other traffic information. The standard aviation communication format — who you're calling, who you are, where you are, and what you want — provides a framework for complete information transmission. Yet, many candidates scramble this sequence or omit critical elements under pressure. Preparation should include practicing radio communications in realistic scenarios, perhaps recording transmissions for self-review or asking instructors to critique communication quality specifically, rather than focusing exclusively on aircraft control. Non-towered airport operations particularly reveal communication proficiency, as candidates must broadcast position reports at appropriate locations using correct phraseology while simultaneously managing aircraft control, traffic scanning, and landing preparation. This multitasking challenge increases when other traffic populates the pattern, requiring pilots to integrate their operations smoothly with existing traffic while maintaining situational awareness about where each aircraft is located and what intentions different pilots have announced.

The psychological dimension of checkride preparation deserves recognition, as managing evaluation anxiety significantly affects performance quality during practical testing. Every candidate experiences nervousness before a checkride; the absence of anxiety would suggest insufficient appreciation of the test's significance. However, productive nervousness that heightens alertness differs fundamentally from debilitating anxiety that degrades performance and disrupts the smooth execution of familiar procedures. The key distinction lies in perception and preparation: candidates who view checkrides as opportunities to demonstrate mastery generally manage stress effectively. In contrast, those who view evaluation as threatening to their judgment tend toward anxiety responses that undermine performance. This perspective shift emerges partly through adequate preparation; pilots genuinely confident in their readiness experience productive nervousness rather than debilitating anxiety, but it also requires conscious cognitive reframing about what checkrides represent. The examiner functions as an expert evaluator assessing whether candidates meet established standards, not as an adversary hoping to identify failures. Most examiners genuinely want candidates to succeed, taking satisfaction in certifying competent pilots rather than identifying deficiencies. Understanding this supportive role helps reframe evaluation anxiety, transforming the examiner from a threatening judge into a professional validator confirming that training has achieved its purpose. Preparation techniques for managing evaluation stress include visualization exercises, imagining successful checkride completion, physical relaxation practices, reducing muscle tension that interferes with smooth control inputs, and cognitive reframing techniques, replacing negative self-talk with realistic capability assessment.

Mock checkrides conducted during the final preparation weeks provide invaluable experience that approximates actual evaluation conditions while allowing errors without certification consequences. These practice evaluations should replicate the real checkride structure as closely as possible, beginning with an oral examination covering aircraft systems, regulations, weather analysis, and performance planning, then proceeding to a comprehensive flight evaluation that includes all maneuvers and procedures the actual practical test will contain. The psychological value of mock checkrides extends beyond identifying technical deficiencies; these practice evaluations reveal how candidates handle evaluation pressure, whether their preparation has achieved genuine readiness, and what mental strategies help manage stress effectively. Many students discover that their first mock checkride performance disappoints compared to their typical training flight quality, revealing how evaluation anxiety affects smoothness of flight and clarity of decision-making. This discovery, while temporarily discouraging, provides essential preparation for managing similar responses during actual evaluation. Subsequent mock checkrides typically show improved stress management as candidates learn that evaluation pressure diminishes with exposure and that performance remains acceptable even when nervousness increases. Using different instructors or designated pilot examiners for mock checkrides provides exposure to various evaluation styles and questioning approaches, reducing the surprise factor when actual examiners use techniques different from those of familiar instructors. Some candidates benefit from conducting mock checkrides at unfamiliar airports, simulating the navigation challenges and facility differences that actual practical tests often involve when designated examiners operate from airports other than candidates' home training facilities.

The final days before the checkride require particular attention to detail and careful planning to maintain proficiency without introducing fatigue or excessive pressure. Many candidates make the mistake of over-practicing immediately before practical tests, flying multiple times daily during the final week in a last-minute preparation frenzy that often degrades performance rather than improving readiness. Aviation skills develop through distributed practice, allowing consolidation between sessions rather than concentrated marathon training that induces fatigue and erodes smooth execution. A better approach involves maintaining a regular flight frequency during the final preparation weeks —perhaps two or three flights per week —while ensuring adequate rest and avoiding physical and mental exhaustion that impairs judgment and coordination. The day before the checkride deserves particular consideration, as some candidates benefit from a brief proficiency flight to confirm readiness, while others find that taking the day off provides better mental preparation through rest. This individual preference varies based on personal stress management strategies and whether recent flying has maintained consistent proficiency or revealed concerning performance variations. The aircraft logbooks, maintenance records, weight-and-balance documentation, and all other required paperwork deserve systematic review during these final days, ensuring that administrative requirements receive the same careful attention as flying proficiency. Checkrides frequently begin with aircraft document review, and deficiencies in required inspections or missing maintenance entries prevent the practical test from being completed, regardless of flying skill. This documentation review includes verifying that the aircraft meets practical test requirements, that appropriate equipment is installed and operational, that required inspections are current, and that no deferred maintenance affects equipment needed for certification evaluation.

The morning of the checkride evaluation arrives with a mixture of anticipation and anxiety that every pilot remembers years later, regardless of how many additional ratings and certificates they subsequently earn. This day represents the culmination of months or years of training, substantial financial investment, countless hours of study and practice, and sustained commitment toward achieving what once seemed an impossible dream. Yet despite the moment's significance, the checkride itself represents simply another flight, another opportunity to demonstrate the skills and knowledge that training has developed into genuine competence. The examiner expects nothing beyond what the Airman Certification Standards explicitly require, no trick questions, no impossible tasks, no subjective judgments based on arbitrary preferences. Candidates who approach practical tests with this realistic perspective, understanding that adequate preparation makes success inevitable rather than uncertain, typically perform well because their confidence remains calibrated to actual capability rather than distorted by either excessive anxiety or dangerous overconfidence. The skills polished during these final preparation weeks serve not just for passing practical tests but throughout aviation careers, establishing habit patterns and proficiency standards that distinguish safe, competent pilots from marginally qualified certificate holders. The checkride, therefore, functions less as an endpoint than as a validation threshold confirming readiness for the real learning that begins after certification, when pilots accept full responsibility for every flight without instructor safety nets protecting against poor decisions or inadequate skill execution. Those who approach checkride preparation with this broader perspective, recognizing that polishing skills for evaluation simultaneously builds capabilities for safe independent operation, invest these final preparation weeks most productively, emerging from successful practical tests not merely with certificates but with genuine confidence that their training has created real competence worthy of the privileges private pilot certification conveys.

The weather briefing process demands heightened attention during checkride preparation, as examiners evaluate not only the ability to obtain weather information but also the interpretive skills needed to make informed go/no-go decisions based on forecast conditions. Many candidates develop abbreviated weather briefing habits during training, relying on instructor judgment about flight feasibility rather than conducting independent analysis of METARs, TAFs, AIRMETs, and other weather products. This dependency becomes problematic during checkride evaluation when candidates must demonstrate autonomous weather assessment capabilities without instructor guidance. Adequate preparation involves conducting comprehensive weather briefings for every flight during the final training weeks and practicing the systematic analysis process required to identify weather hazards and determine whether conditions support safe flight within personal and regulatory limitations. The examiner expects candidates to recognize weather patterns suggesting potential deterioration during planned flight duration, identify frontal passages that might affect return flights even when departure conditions appear acceptable, and understand prognostic charts well enough to visualize how current weather systems will evolve throughout the day.

Weather-related decision scenarios frequently challenge candidates during oral examinations, requiring assessment of hypothetical situations in which forecast conditions are marginal or the potential for weather changes during flight exists. These scenarios test judgment more than weather theory knowledge. Can candidates recognize situations requiring conservative decisions even when regulatory requirements might technically permit flight? The distinction between legal and safe becomes critically important, as weather conditions can satisfy minimum VFR requirements while presenting risks exceeding prudent personal limitations. Checkride preparation should include analyzing recent weather scenarios, determining what decisions would have been appropriate given forecast conditions, and comparing actual weather to predictions. This retrospective analysis builds the pattern-recognition skills necessary for anticipating weather developments and identifying situations where forecast uncertainty warrants extra caution or alternative planning. Candidates who approach weather assessment as an exercise in legal minimums miss the deeper judgment dimension that experienced pilots develop, the intuitive recognition that certain weather patterns, even when technically legal, present risks not commensurate with the mission's importance or the pilot's experience level.

Chapter 11: The Day of Reckoning: Earning the Wings

The morning arrives as usual, yet everything feels fundamentally different. The alarm sounds in darkness, pulling consciousness from dreams where flight maneuvers replay endlessly in perfect execution. Rising from bed brings the sharp awareness that today marks the culmination of months, perhaps years, of dedication, expense, study, and practice. Today is checkride day —the practical examination in which the Federal Aviation Administration's designated examiner will determine whether competence justifies certification or whether additional training remains necessary. The weight of this reality settles across shoulders like a physical presence as the day begins, transforming routine morning activities into surreal experiences where ordinary actions feel strangely disconnected from consciousness focused entirely on the evaluation ahead.

The drive to the airport occurs in a temporal distortion where minutes simultaneously drag and accelerate, traffic lights seeming to conspire against timely arrival, while the destination approaches too quickly. Inside the vehicle, mental rehearsal continues the pattern established during weeks of final preparation, reviewing emergency procedures, reciting V-speeds, visualizing approach patterns, and mentally flying through maneuvers that must demonstrate precision earned through countless repetitions. Yet this rehearsal carries different stakes now. No instructor will provide corrective guidance during the examination flight. No opportunity exists to repeat a maneuver that fails to meet standards. The examiner will witness performance exactly as it unfolds, making judgments based upon regulatory standards that permit no negotiation or subjective interpretation. This reality creates a peculiar psychological state where confidence battles doubt, where genuine competence confronts imposter syndrome, whispering that perhaps preparation remains insufficient despite evidence to the contrary.

Arriving at the aviation facility immediately immerses you in the day's formalities. The examiner, likely someone encountered only briefly during pre-checkride coordination, appears professional and cordial yet maintains an appropriate distance from casual friendliness. This dynamic serves important regulatory purposes; the evaluation must remain objective and standardized, uninfluenced by personal relationships or emotional appeals. Some examiners project stern demeanors suggesting harsh evaluation standards, while others adopt warmer approaches designed to reduce anxiety and encourage natural performance. Regardless of stylistic differences, all examiners share the fundamental responsibility of serving as gatekeepers, ensuring that only qualified pilots receive certification and are allowed to carry passengers into the skies, where mistakes cost lives. Understanding this responsibility helps contextualize the examination process not as adversarial confrontation but as necessary verification that training produced genuine competence worthy of public trust.

The oral examination commences in a conference room or office, where documents are spread across tables and aviation knowledge is systematically evaluated. This phase, often lasting three to five hours, covers the vast theoretical foundation underlying practical piloting skills, aerodynamics principles, weather theory, aircraft systems, regulations, aeronautical decision-making, and countless other topics that transform intuitive stick-and-rudder skills into professional aviator competence. The examiner's questions probe not merely rote memorization but genuine understanding, asking candidates to explain concepts in their own words, to analyze scenarios requiring judgment, and to demonstrate the ability to locate information in appropriate references when specific details escape immediate recall. This distinction between knowing facts and understanding principles becomes immediately apparent as questions progress beyond simple recall toward application and analysis.

Some questions arrive as expected, covering topics emphasized during ground school and instructor briefings, airspace classifications, weather minimums, required equipment, and performance calculations familiar from countless practice sessions. Other questions surprise, exploring edge cases or unusual scenarios that reveal whether understanding extends beyond prepared talking points into genuine comprehension. An examiner might ask about the behavior of the electrical system during alternator failure, requiring candidates to trace power flow through backup systems and identify which components continue operating and which become inoperative. Another question might present a hypothetical situation involving marginal weather, deteriorating visibility, and uncertain fuel reserves, asking candidates to discuss decision-making processes and available options. These scenario-based questions evaluate aeronautical decision-making capabilities that distinguish safe pilots from those who merely possess technical knowledge without the judgment needed to apply it appropriately.

Throughout the oral examination, candidates discover how preparation shapes confidence and performance. Those who studied systematically, understanding concepts rather than memorizing isolated facts, navigate questions smoothly, recognizing patterns connecting seemingly disparate topics. Regulation questions connect to practical operations, weather theory links to actual decision-making scenarios, and aircraft systems knowledge enables troubleshooting hypothetical malfunctions. Conversely, preparation gaps become painfully obvious as questions expose areas where understanding remains superficial or incomplete. The examiner might pause after an uncertain response, allowing candidates time to reconsider answers or consult references. This grace period acknowledges that examination stress affects recall and that pilots need not possess encyclopedic knowledge instantly accessible without thought. What matters more than perfect recall is demonstrating appropriate thought processes, knowing where to find information when uncertain, and showing awareness of knowledge limitations rather than fabricating confident-sounding answers to mask ignorance.

The aircraft logbook review constitutes another critical examination phase in which documentation is scrutinized to determine whether training followed proper procedures and whether the aircraft's maintenance status permits legal operation. The examiner reviews annual inspections, transponder certifications, pitot-static checks, ELT battery replacements, and countless other maintenance actions mandated by regulations. Airworthiness directives receive particular attention, with examiners verifying that manufacturers' mandatory safety modifications and recurring inspections have been completed and adequately documented. Any documentation discrepancies discovered during this review can halt the examination immediately; even perfect flying performance cannot overcome operating an aircraft that fails to meet airworthiness requirements. This logbook scrutiny teaches valuable lessons about regulatory compliance extending beyond personal piloting skills into aircraft oversight responsibilities that private pilots must understand.

Similarly, the pilot's logbook undergoes a detailed examination, during which the examiner verifies that the minimum 40 hours of training, including specified dual instruction, solo flight time, cross-country experience, instrument training, and night operations, mandated by regulations before private pilot certification, have been satisfied. Beyond merely counting hours, examiners verify that authorized instructors properly complete required endorsements, that training addresses all necessary areas, and that experience meets not just minimums but also demonstrates reasonable competence development. Some candidates arrive with exactly the minimum required hours, having progressed efficiently through training without significant setbacks. Others present logbooks showing substantially more experience, perhaps reflecting learning challenges requiring additional instruction or conservative instructor standards that demand proficiency beyond the bare minimums needed for certification. Neither pattern necessarily predicts examination success; what matters is demonstrating current competence that meets standards, regardless of how many hours the journey took.

The transition from ground evaluation to flight examination brings both relief and heightened anxiety. Relief comes from completing the oral phase successfully and from surviving hours of questioning without encountering knowledge gaps that require discontinuing the test. Heightened anxiety stems from recognizing that the practical demonstration now determines the outcome, that theoretical knowledge must now translate into physical performance, and that mistakes become immediately visible rather than hidden within mental processes. Walking toward the aircraft brings a peculiar awareness of being observed, of having every action evaluated from the initial approach through preflight inspection. Does the candidate systematically walk around, checking all required items? Do control surface movements receive proper attention? Does the fuel sump drain procedure capture all potential contamination locations? These seemingly mundane actions demonstrate professionalism and thoroughness that examiners note carefully, recognizing that pilots who rush through preflight inspections or skip steps compromise safety before engines even start.

Inside the cockpit, the familiar environment feels transformed by the examiner's presence in the right seat. The same instruments, controls, and systems used during hundreds of training hours are now subjected to official scrutiny, where every action contributes to the evaluation outcome. Engine start procedures follow the checklist exactly, with the examiner noting whether the candidate demonstrates proper technique or exhibits unsafe shortcuts. Radio communications receive particular attention as initial contact with ground control and clearance delivery reveals whether the candidate can function effectively within the controlled airspace, communicating clearly and following instructions accurately. Some candidates discover that examination pressure affects radio work dramatically, causing usually articulate speakers to stumble over standard phraseology or misunderstand simple instructions. Recognizing this stress response and deliberately slowing communication pace helps maintain clarity despite nervous energy coursing through every interaction.

The flight examination portion unfolds through a predetermined sequence of tasks that examiners select from the applicable practical test standards, the regulatory document specifying minimum performance criteria for private pilot certification. Takeoff must demonstrate proper crosswind technique when wind conditions warrant, with the aircraft tracking the centerline throughout the roll and establishing an appropriate climb speed and attitude during the initial ascent. Departure procedures must follow any assigned routing or clearances, with proper traffic pattern exits and airspace awareness, preventing conflicts with other aircraft or unauthorized entries into controlled sectors. Each maneuver receives an introduction from the examiner specifying the parameters, altitude, heading, and configuration, followed by the candidate's execution, which demonstrates proficiency. Steep turns must maintain altitude within 100 feet while banking 45 degrees and rolling smoothly from one direction into the opposite turn. Slow flight requires maintaining steady altitude and heading while operating at minimum controllable airspeed, where control responsiveness becomes mushy and stall warning systems activate persistently.

Power-off stalls replicate approach-to-landing scenarios in which improper speed management allows airspeed to decay below the minimum sustainable flight speed, requiring immediate recognition and recovery while minimizing altitude loss. Power-on stalls simulate departure situations in which excessive pitch attitude during climb produces an aerodynamic condition that demands a different recovery technique. Emergency procedures interrupt normal flight operations unexpectedly, with the examiner suddenly pulling the throttle to idle and announcing engine failure, requiring immediate response, establishing best glide speed, identifying suitable emergency landing locations, completing emergency checklists, and demonstrating the decision-making necessary if engine power cannot be restored. These simulated emergencies produce some of the examination's most stressful moments because they demand integrating multiple skills simultaneously — aircraft control, emergency procedure recall, aeronautical decision-making, and communication — while processing the psychological impact of simulated catastrophic failure.

Navigation tasks evaluate piloting skills in realistic operational contexts where multiple demands compete for attention simultaneously. The examiner might request diversion to an alternate airport, requiring candidates to identify the destination on charts, determine the appropriate heading and distance, establish navigation tracking, and monitor progress while maintaining altitude, airspeed, and traffic awareness. Ground reference maneuvers demonstrate precise aircraft control at low altitude, where wind effects become pronounced and accurate position maintenance requires continuous control adjustments. Turning around a point requires circular paths, maintaining a constant radius from a ground reference despite wind pushing the aircraft toward or away from the center, demanding bank angle variations and continuous situational awareness. S-turns across roads mandate semicircular reversing paths that test wind-correction judgment and spatial visualization as the aircraft transitions from downwind to upwind segments, requiring dramatically different bank angles to maintain proper ground-track geometry.

The return to the airport for landing practice shifts the focus to operations where precision matters most. Pattern entry must demonstrate proper spacing behind existing traffic, appropriate communication with tower controllers if operating at controlled fields, and correct positioning for downwind leg establishment. The base-to-final turn receives particular examiner attention because this transition presents significant accident potential: pilots may lose situational awareness, stall during steeply banked turns while attempting to correct alignment problems, or fail to maintain traffic vigilance while concentrating on approach setup. The first landing might be normal, demonstrating standard approach procedures in which everything proceeds as routine. Subsequent landings add complexity, with short-field approaches requiring precise speed control and minimum landing distance, soft-field techniques demanding gentle touchdowns with weight gradually transferring to the landing gear, or crosswind approaches necessitating specialized control inputs to maintain runway alignment despite wind attempting to weathervane the aircraft.

Each landing produces immediate performance feedback impossible to disguise or rationalize. Touchdowns either occur smoothly with centerline alignment and proper speed dissipation, or they reveal deficiencies through bounced landings, ballooned approaches, side loads indicating incomplete crosswind correction, or long floats consuming excessive runway distance. The examiner silently absorbs these observations, providing no immediate indication of whether performance meets standards or requires demonstration improvement through additional attempts. This ambiguity creates psychological pressure as the flight examination progresses. Without feedback confirming success or indicating failure, candidates remain uncertain about overall performance, unable to determine whether they're comfortably exceeding standards or barely meeting minimums. Some interpret the examiner's silence as approval, assuming that unsatisfactory performance would prompt immediate intervention. Others view silence as ominous, worrying that the examiner is documenting deficiencies for post-flight discussion, which may culminate in examination failure.

The flight examination concludes when the examiner determines that all required tasks have received adequate evaluation, with the aircraft returning to parking and engines securing for the final time under examination conditions. The post-flight discussion begins immediately or after brief documentation is completed, during which the examiner reviews notes and completes paperwork recording the examination outcome. These moments are interminable as candidates await the verdict, determining whether months of effort culminate in certification or disappointing failure requiring additional training before retesting. The examiner's expression reveals little, maintaining a professional demeanor as they review performance across all evaluated areas. Some examiners provide detailed debriefing covering both strengths and weaknesses observed throughout the examination, while others deliver succinct summaries focused primarily on outcome determination.

When the examiner extends congratulations and confirmation of successful completion, relief washes over newly certificated pilots with almost physical intensity. The transformation feels both momentous and anticlimactic, despite years of dreaming about this moment, despite months of intensive training toward this goal; the actual certification arrives through a simple declaration rather than a dramatic ceremony. The temporary airman certificate, printed on ordinary paper, hardly seems worthy of the accomplishment it represents. Yet, this document carries the Federal Aviation Administration's authority, granting privileges that transform the holder from a supervised student into an autonomous pilot authorized to carry passengers and conduct flights without oversight. The examiner typically shares a perspective on pilot responsibility, reminding newly certificated aviators that certification represents not mastery but rather demonstration of the minimum competence necessary for continued learning. Real education begins now, during subsequent flights where no instructor safety net exists and where judgment must protect against the countless scenarios that training could never fully anticipate.

The opposite outcome, notification of unsuccessful completion, produces crushing disappointment that temporarily overshadows rational understanding that most pilots who eventually earn certification fail at least one checkride attempt. The examiner identifies specific areas where performance did not meet standards, distinguishing minor deficiencies that require brief additional practice from significant gaps that require comprehensive remediation. Some failures stem from a single critical error — such as an unstabilized approach leading to a go-around refusal and a dangerous landing attempt, a regulatory violation demonstrating inadequate understanding of airspace, or an emergency procedure response revealing incomplete preparation. Other failures reflect broader competence concerns, with multiple tasks revealing consistent performance deficiencies, suggesting that fundamental skill development remains incomplete. Regardless of the specifics of the failure, the experience teaches valuable lessons about the importance of preparation, pressure management, and the reality that certification standards exist not as arbitrary obstacles but as necessary minimums to ensure aviation safety.

The aftermath of a checkride, whether successful or not, involves emotional processing as adrenaline dissipates and the experience is given conscious reflection. Successful candidates often report feeling simultaneously elated and deflated, thrilled by accomplishment yet struggling with the sudden absence of the long-pursued goal that provided structure and purpose for months. The achievement that seemed impossibly distant during early training stages now exists as accomplished reality, raising questions about what comes next. Some immediately begin planning aviation adventures now possible with certification, imagining weekend flights to distant airports, scenic tours sharing flight with family and friends, or continued training toward advanced ratings and capabilities. Others feel unexpected anxiety recognizing that instructor safety nets no longer exist, that subsequent flights occur without oversight, ensuring that decisions remain sound and techniques stay proficient.

The first post-certification flight without an examiner or instructor aboard carries symbolic weight as the inaugural exercise of newly earned privileges. This flight might be simple, perhaps just pattern practice at the familiar home airport, performing landings and takeoffs that reestablish routine after examination pressure. Or it might be ambitious, a cross-country journey to destinations discussed hypothetically throughout training but now accessible through actual authority rather than supervised permission. Either approach is valid; what matters is recognizing that private pilot certification represents a beginning rather than a conclusion, that competence requires maintenance through regular practice and continued learning, and that aviation safety depends on honest self-assessment, distinguishing comfortable capabilities from situations exceeding current proficiency.

The broader significance of private pilot certification extends beyond personal achievement into joining a community spanning aviation history from the Wright brothers through countless pilots who transformed flight from experimental novelty into routine capability. The certificate carries obligations alongside privileges: responsibility for passengers who trust certified pilots with their lives, a duty to operate safely within a system serving millions of travelers daily, and a commitment to maintaining proficiency and judgment worthy of the privileges granted. Some newly certificated pilots struggle with imposter syndrome, questioning whether they truly possess the competence that certification supposedly validates. This doubt, while uncomfortable, serves a valuable purpose by maintaining healthy respect for aviation's inherent risks and preventing the overconfidence that turns competent pilots into accident statistics. The balance between confidence, which enables an enjoyable flight, and caution, which prevents dangerous situations, defines airmanship throughout aviation careers, beginning with private pilot certification.

Looking forward to certification day, the aviation journey now extends infinitely across horizons accessible through earned qualification. Some pilots view private certification as sufficient accomplishment, pursuing aviation purely for recreation without aspirations toward advanced ratings or professional flying careers. They may fly occasionally for weekend excursions or maintain currency simply for the satisfaction of capability retention, finding fulfillment in the freedom that private pilot privileges provide. Others see private certification as a foundation for continued advancement, toward instrument ratings enabling flight through clouds and adverse weather, commercial certificates authorizing compensation for piloting services, and instructor certifications allowing others to teach the skills so recently mastered. Both paths honor the achievement represented by that temporary certificate issued following successful checkride completion, and both require the ongoing dedication, judgment, and respect for aviation complexity that training instilled throughout the certification journey.

The day of reckoning that initially loomed as an intimidating ordeal ultimately reveals itself as appropriate verification that preparation transformed dreams into genuine capability, that the person who could barely maintain altitude during early training flights developed into a pilot meeting Federal Aviation Administration standards for certificated airman privileges. The checkride's challenges, the comprehensive oral examination, the systematic evaluation of flight maneuvers, and the pressure of performing without a safety net or second chances serve essential purposes, ensuring that certification carries meaning beyond participation trophy acknowledgment. Pilots who earn wings through examination, meeting rigorous standards, gain not merely paperwork permission but legitimate competence, justifying the trust that passengers, fellow pilots, and regulatory authorities place in those holding private pilot certificates. This legitimacy transforms certification from bureaucratic formality into genuine accomplishment worthy of pride, while simultaneously establishing the foundation for continued growth throughout aviation journeys that extend far beyond that momentous day when an examiner's congratulations confirmed that skyward dreams had become a reality.

The weeks immediately following certification bring a unique period of adjustment, during which newfound freedom intermingles with lingering uncertainty about exercising privileges without supervision. The psychological transition from student to certificated pilot occurs gradually rather than instantly, despite the official status change documented on that temporary certificate. Many new pilots find themselves mentally consulting absent instructors before decisions that fall squarely within their own judgment authority, wondering whether weather conditions justify flight, whether crosswind components exceed comfortable limits, or whether unfamiliar airports present challenges beyond current capabilities. This internal consultation process reflects healthy caution rather than weakness, demonstrating awareness that certification validates minimum standards rather than conferring omniscience about every aviation scenario.

The first solo passenger flight represents a particularly significant milestone that amplifies responsibility in ways that training flights never quite captured. When a friend or family member settles into the right seat previously occupied by instructors and examiners, the weight of their trust becomes tangible. They cannot evaluate whether preflight procedures were sufficiently thorough, whether the weather assessment properly considered all relevant factors, or whether the pilot's technique meets safe standards. They trust the certificate, assuming that regulatory oversight ensures competence worthy of their confidence. This trust demands reciprocal responsibility, honest assessment of conditions, conservative decision-making that prioritizes safety over schedule or pride, and a willingness to cancel or postpone flights when circumstances exceed comfort levels. Some pilots discover that carrying passengers produces anxiety, interfering with normal performance, creating feedback loops where nervousness degrades flying quality, which increases anxiety further. Recognizing this pattern and deliberately practicing passenger flights helps normalize the experience until additional occupants enhance rather than compromise flying enjoyment.

Weather decision-making evolves significantly during post-certification flights, when no instructor provides second opinions, leaving go/no-go assessments to stand or fall on their own. Student pilots often deferred to the instructor's judgment, accepting weather decisions without fully developing independent evaluation skills. Certificated pilots must cultivate personal minimums exceeding regulatory requirements, self-imposed limits on crosswind components, visibility requirements, ceiling heights, and other factors that training revealed as challenging. These personal minimums might initially exceed legal minimums by a significant margin, perhaps requiring visibility twice the regulatory standard or avoiding solo flight entirely during gusty conditions. As experience accumulates and proficiency increases, personal minimums can gradually relax toward regulatory limits, though truly prudent pilots maintain margins, recognizing that legal minimums represent emergency tolerances rather than comfortable operating conditions.

Aircraft rental dynamics also shift after certification, as pilots transition from training scheduling, where instructors coordinated availability, to independent reservation systems in which personal judgment determines appropriate flight frequency. Financial considerations exert greater influence now that dual instruction costs no longer apply; Hobbs meter hours accumulate more slowly when budgets cannot absorb unlimited flying expenses. This economic reality creates proficiency challenges for pilots lacking funds for frequent flying. Skills atrophy rapidly without regular practice, particularly landing techniques that require precise coordination and emergency procedures that demand immediate, correct responses. Pilots flying monthly or less frequently must honestly assess whether proficiency remains adequate or whether skill degradation justifies limiting operations until practice flights restore capabilities. Some establish recurrent training programs with instructors, scheduling periodic flight reviews beyond minimum regulatory requirements to identify and address developing weaknesses before they compromise safety.

The aviation community provides invaluable support during this post-certification adjustment period through flying clubs, pilot associations, and informal mentorship relationships. Experienced pilots who remember their own certification transitions often generously share wisdom accumulated through years of flights, encountering situations that training never addressed. They describe decision-making processes that kept them safe when conditions deteriorated unexpectedly, explain techniques for managing passenger expectations and anxieties, and offer encouragement when new pilots struggle with confidence or proficiency concerns. Airport pilot lounges become classrooms where hangar flying, verbal replays of notable flights, and lessons learned transmit institutional knowledge, supplementing formal training. These conversations reveal that even pilots with thousands of hours continue learning, continue making occasional mistakes, and continue respecting aviation's capacity for humbling even experienced aviators who momentarily forget that complacency invites consequences.

The checkride day ultimately reveals itself as a beginning rather than a conclusion, a gateway marking the transition from supervised student to autonomous pilot, accepting full responsibility for decisions that formal training prepared for without fully insulating against aviation's inherent uncertainties. The temporary certificate issued following successful examination represents not mastery but instead society's trust that demonstrated competence justifies self-directed continued learning throughout flying careers extending decades beyond that pivotal day when an examiner's approval transformed dreams into documented reality. Understanding this perspective frames certification appropriately, neither minimizing the genuine accomplishment nor inflating it beyond its actual significance as one milestone among many throughout aviation journeys limited only by dedication, judgment, and the endless horizons beckoning those privileged to slip the surly bonds of earth and dance the skies on laughter-silvered wings.

Chapter 12: Beyond the License: Embracing a Lifetime of Flight

The temporary certificate emerging from the examiner's printer represents simultaneously an ending and a beginning, a paradox that takes years to appreciate fully. With ink still settling on that precious document authorizing solo flight without supervision, new certificated pilots often experience disorientation equal to anything encountered during hooded instrument training. The structure that defined existence for months suddenly dissolves, no instructor scheduling the next lesson, no syllabus dictating what skills require development, no examiner looming as an imminent checkpoint requiring preparation. This absence of external direction initially feels liberating —a hard-won freedom to explore aviation on personal terms and at one's own schedule. Yet within weeks, many pilots discover something unsettling. Without structured guidance, their flying activities diminish rather than expand, the license gathering dust while life's competing demands reclaim attention previously devoted to training. The certificate that seemed like a destination reveals itself as merely a beginning point, and the real challenge emerges not in earning the privilege to fly but in maintaining and expanding that privilege through decades of continuous engagement with aviation's ever-evolving demands.

The first few flights after certification carry a unique psychological weight that distinguishes them from any previous aviation experience. During training, even solo flights operated within established boundaries, geographic limitations, and implicit instructor oversight, the knowledge that someone would review logbook entries, hear about challenges encountered, and provide guidance for improvement. Now, for the first time, genuine autonomy prevails. The decision to fly rests entirely on personal judgment; the destinations are constrained only by aircraft capability and regulatory boundaries; the conduct of each flight is visible to no authority unless something goes wrong. This newfound freedom initially produces cautiousness bordering on paralysis for many pilots, who suddenly recognize how much confidence was derived from knowing instructors would catch errors before they cascaded into danger. The first passengers carried, often family members eager to experience flight with their newly certified pilot, introduced pressures absent during training, when only the instructor's life depended on competent decision-making. These inaugural post-certification flights teach essential lessons about personal responsibility that no training curriculum adequately captures, revealing that the examiner's approval certified minimum competence rather than complete readiness for aviation's infinite variety of situations and challenges.

Currency and proficiency, terms often confused or used interchangeably, represent distinct concepts that become critically important once the training's regular rhythm disappears. Currency describes legal requirements, the regulations specifying how many takeoffs and landings within what time period permit carrying passengers, the biennial flight review mandating instructor assessment every twenty-four months, and the medical certificate expiration dates determining authorization to exercise pilot privileges. These regulatory minimums establish floors below which operation becomes illegal, bright lines that cannot be crossed without consequences. Proficiency, conversely, represents the actual skill level —the genuine capability to safely execute maneuvers and manage situations that might arise during flight. While currency can be maintained through minimum compliance — three takeoffs and landings to a complete stop within ninety days for carrying passengers during daytime conditions — proficiency requires more substantial engagement with aviation, consistent practice that keeps skills sharp, and decision-making capabilities honed. The newly certificated pilot who flies exactly once every eighty-nine days to maintain currency while letting proficiency erode creates dangerous illusions of capability, holding a valid certificate and meeting legal requirements while actually operating with diminished skills that haven't faced real challenge since the checkride weeks or months previous. Understanding this distinction is essential for managing aviation safety throughout a flying career, developing personal minimums that exceed regulatory requirements to ensure currency and proficiency remain aligned rather than diverge into dangerous gaps between legal authorization and actual capability.

Financial realities impose harsh constraints on aviation dreams as training costs are only partially revealed. During certification pursuit, expenses seemed purposeful, each dollar spent moving measurably toward the goal of examiner approval. The hourly aircraft rental rates, instructor fees, knowledge test expenses, and checkride costs accumulated toward something tangible, a certificate authorizing independent flight. Once earned, however, aviation expenses become discretionary costs competing with mortgages, retirement savings, children's education funds, and countless other financial demands that adult life imposes. The aircraft that seemed reasonably priced during training — perhaps 150 dollars per hour, including fuel — reveals its actual cost when calculated over the flying frequency required to maintain genuine proficiency. Even modest activity levels of four hours monthly generate nearly two thousand dollars in annual direct costs, without accounting for insurance, hangar or tiedown fees if ownership seems attractive, headset replacements, chart subscriptions, medical examination expenses, biennial flight review costs, and the steady stream of incidental expenses that aviation inevitably generates. Many newly certificated pilots experience a painful awakening during their first year of licensed flight, discovering that maintaining meaningful engagement with aviation requires a financial commitment equal to or exceeding what training demanded, now spread indefinitely across years rather than concentrated into the finite period until checkride completion. This economic reality explains why substantial percentages of certificated pilots become inactive within five years, their dreams grounded not by loss of interest but by honest assessment that aviation cannot justify its costs against competing financial priorities in lives where resources remain limited and choices require difficult prioritization.

The aviation community offers resources and structures that successful long-term pilots learn to leverage, replacing the formal training environment with informal networks that sustain engagement and support continuous development. Flying clubs provide both economic advantages through shared aircraft ownership costs and social benefits through regular interaction with fellow pilots whose experiences and perspectives enrich personal aviation knowledge. The pilot who flies solo, never engaging with other aviators beyond the minimum necessary interactions during fuel stops and tower communications, misses opportunities for learning that exceed what any single individual can accumulate through isolated experience. Hangar talk, often dismissed as mere storytelling or even dangerous perpetuation of bad habits, actually serves essential educational functions when approached critically. Listening to how other pilots managed unexpected weather encounters, dealt with mechanical anomalies, navigated unfamiliar airspace, or handled emergencies provides vicarious learning that expands personal knowledge without requiring direct experience of every possible challenge aviation presents. The key lies in developing discrimination, recognizing which stories contain genuinely helpful lessons versus which reflect dangerous attitudes or illegal activities deserving condemnation rather than emulation. Organizations like the Aircraft Owners and Pilots Association, Experimental Aircraft Association, and specialized groups focusing on particular aircraft types, mission profiles, or geographic regions create communities where pilots find both social connection and practical support. These networks prove especially valuable when aircraft maintenance issues arise, questions about insurance or aircraft ownership surface, or when seeking recommendations for instructors capable of providing specialized training in areas such as tailwheel operations, aerobatics, or advanced navigation techniques.

Ongoing education distinguishes pilots who thrive throughout decades of flying from those who stagnate with checkride-level skills gradually eroding toward incompetence. The private pilot certificate represents merely the first step in a training hierarchy that extends through instrument ratings, commercial certificates, multiengine endorsements, and ultimately airline transport pilot certification for those pursuing professional careers. Even pilots without airline aspirations benefit tremendously from pursuing advanced training, particularly instrument rating acquisition, which transforms aviation from fair-weather recreation into practical transportation capable of maintaining a reliable schedule. The decision to seek additional ratings immediately rather than wait until financial situations improve or life circumstances permit presents difficult trade-offs. Continuing directly from private certification into instrument training maintains momentum, preserves knowledge that might otherwise decay, and establishes regular flying patterns that are harder to resume once interrupted. However, consolidating private pilot skills through extensive visual flight operations before adding the complexity of instrument training allows for a more profound mastery of fundamental aircraft control and decision-making without the task saturation that instrument flying introduces. Some pilots benefit from intermediate steps such as pursuing complex or high-performance endorsements, acquiring tailwheel experience that refines aircraft control on more challenging platforms, or obtaining seaplane ratings that combine adventure with genuine skill development. These varied pathways prevent aviation from becoming routine, introducing novel challenges that rekindle the excitement of initial training while building genuine capability across diverse operational environments.

Flight safety seminars and accident analysis provide education that extends beyond aircraft control skills into the judgment domain where most aviation incidents originate. The Aircraft Owners and Pilots Association's Air Safety Institute produces exceptional educational materials examining actual accidents, extracting lessons that help pilots recognize dangerous patterns before replicating them. These resources address not just technical failures but the human factors, cognitive biases, and decision-making errors that lead competent pilots into situations where skills prove insufficient for survival. The newly certificated pilot who studies accident reports often experiences unsettling recognition of how easily circumstances combine to trap well-meaning aviators in deteriorating situations. Reading how pilots continued visual flight into instrument meteorological conditions despite mounting evidence of worsening weather, how pilots attempted operations in high-density altitude conditions without adequately calculating performance capabilities, and how pilots proceeded with flights despite mechanical discrepancies they rationalized as minor, these accounts illuminate the gap between knowledge and judgment, between understanding theoretical hazards and recognizing them unfolding in real time. Regular engagement with safety materials cultivates the habit of critical self-assessment, the willingness to question personal decisions, and the ability to identify early warning signs that situations are developing in directions better abandoned than persisted through toward potential disaster. This safety-focused education proves more valuable than additional maneuver practice for preventing the accidents that kill pilots with hundreds or thousands of hours who possess adequate stick-and-rudder skills but insufficient judgment about when to exercise them.

Mentorship relationships, whether formalized or organic, provide guidance that accelerates development while helping newer pilots avoid common pitfalls that claim experience and sometimes lives. The newly certificated pilot who cultivates relationships with experienced aviators gains access to decades of accumulated wisdom that no amount of independent flying can generate within reasonable timeframes. These mentor relationships differ fundamentally from instructor-student dynamics that characterized training, operating instead as collegial exchanges in which more experienced pilots share insights while respecting the growing expertise of newer aviators, whose fresh perspectives sometimes illuminate habitual practices worth reconsidering. The ideal mentor combines extensive experience with communication skills and a genuine interest in developing other pilots' capabilities rather than simply impressing them with personal accomplishments. Finding such mentors requires initiative, attending aviation social events, participating in club activities, volunteering for airport improvement projects, and demonstrating the seriousness of purpose that motivates experienced pilots to invest time in others' development. These relationships prove especially valuable during decision-making crossroads: whether to purchase versus rent aircraft, which avionics upgrades justify their expense, how to approach particular training goals, and how to interpret regulations whose language admits multiple reasonable interpretations. A trusted mentor provides reality-checking that prevents expensive mistakes while encouraging appropriate risk-taking that expands capabilities without crossing into dangerous territory. The wisdom to know which risks merit acceptance versus which deserve avoidance often separates pilots who enjoy long, rewarding aviation careers from those whose flying ends prematurely through accidents, incidents, or abandonment after frightening near-misses that could have been prevented with better guidance.

Aircraft ownership represents a dream for many pilots and a practical decision for others whose flying frequency justifies the financial and administrative burdens it entails. The transition from renter to owner fundamentally changes aviation relationships, creating both opportunities and obligations that renting never imposed. Owners enjoy unparalleled freedom: aircraft available whenever desired, without scheduling conflicts; the capability to leave personal items secured in storage compartments; the freedom to upgrade avionics or modify interiors according to individual preferences; and the elimination of restrictions on where aircraft can be flown or how long trips can be. These advantages come with substantial responsibilities that extend well beyond purchase prices. Annual inspections, periodic equipment certifications, hangar or tiedown costs, insurance premiums reflecting liability and hull coverage decisions, maintenance reserve funds for inevitable repair expenses, and the administrative burden of tracking airworthiness directives and equipment life limits consume time and money that renting never required contemplating. The decision to pursue ownership demands an honest assessment of flying frequency and mission requirements that might justify the economics of ownership. A pilot flying 5 hours per month probably cannot justify owning the aircraft alone. In contrast, a pilot regularly flying 8 or 10 hours monthly might find ownership more economical than renting, while gaining scheduling flexibility and aircraft familiarity that enhance safety and convenience. Partnership arrangements and flying clubs offer middle-ground solutions that share ownership burdens among multiple pilots while providing many ownership advantages. The aircraft selection process itself involves complex decisions that balance performance, efficiency, acquisition cost, operating expenses, and mission suitability. The high-performance single-engine aircraft that seems ideal for long-distance trips might prove unnecessarily expensive and complex for local flying, which comprises most actual operations. At the same time, the economic trainer might lack the capability for trips that initially seemed rare but eventually become routine. Successful aircraft ownership requires making decisions analytically rather than emotionally. However, the passion that draws people to aviation inevitably colors even the most rigorous financial analysis with optimistic assumptions about flying frequency and mission requirements.

Technology continuously reshapes aviation, creating both opportunities and challenges for pilots navigating the transition from certification to long-term flying careers. The panel-mounted GPS navigators and electronic flight displays that seemed sophisticated during training represent only the beginning of a technological revolution that will transform navigation, communication, and decision-making. Portable devices running aviation applications provide capabilities that recently required tens of thousands of dollars in permanently installed avionics, moving maps displaying real-time position, weather imagery updating via internet connections, traffic information revealing nearby aircraft, terrain warnings preventing controlled flight into ground, instrument approach plates eliminating chart subscription expenses, and weight-and-balance calculators that simplify pre-flight planning. These technologies deliver undeniable benefits, providing access to information and situational awareness that previous generations of pilots never imagined. However, technology introduces dependencies and creates vulnerabilities that merit serious consideration. The pilot who never practices pilotage and dead reckoning because GPS always provides precise navigation loses fundamental skills that might prove essential if electrical failures render all panel-mounted and portable devices inoperative. The pilot who relies exclusively on datalink weather displays might miss visible evidence that conditions are deteriorating faster than updates reflect, or might develop false confidence that comprehensive weather information eliminates the need for conservative decision-making when uncertainty exists. Technology proves most valuable for pilots who master fundamental skills first, then add electronic capabilities as supplements rather than replacements for basic knowledge. The newly certificated pilot benefits from deliberately flying some trips using only a chart and compass, calculating winds from ground-speed observations and course corrections, and practicing navigation techniques that remain valid when sophisticated systems fail. This foundation ensures that technology enhances capabilities without creating brittle dependencies that lead to dangerous situations when systems fail, rather than mere inconveniences that require fallback to traditional methods.

Mission definition evolves continuously throughout flying careers, requiring periodic reassessment of how aviation fits within broader life contexts and whether aircraft capabilities, pilot skills, and operational approaches align with actual rather than imagined missions. Many pilots pursue certification with vague notions of using aviation for business travel, weekend getaways to fascinating destinations, or simply the freedom to explore at will. Reality often diverges from these initial visions as practical constraints, weather limitations, and life circumstances shape actual flying activities. The business executive who imagined using personal aircraft for client visits might discover that weather uncertainty makes aviation unreliable for time-critical appointments, or that the convenience of direct routing rarely overcomes the hassle of arranging ground transportation at destinations. The pilot who envisioned regular family trips to distant vacation spots might find that passengers tolerate turbulence poorly, that coordinating schedules around weather becomes more frustrating than planning around airline timetables, or that automobile trips offer advantages, with spontaneous stops and diversions that make journeys memorable. Conversely, some pilots discover unexpected aviation applications that never factored into initial certification decisions. The landscape photographer finds that aerial perspectives create unique images impossible to capture from ground level. The volunteer discovers that humanitarian organizations desperately need pilots willing to transport medical supplies, transplant organs, or patients to treatment centers. The aircraft owner realizes that providing instruction, though never part of original flying plans, offers both financial benefits and deep satisfaction from helping others achieve aviation dreams. These mission evolutions require honesty about whether current aircraft ownership, rating limitations, or skill levels support actual flying activities versus those imagined initially. The pilot flying exclusively within one hundred miles of home base gains little from maintaining high-performance aircraft capable of crossing continents, while the pilot regularly making four-hundred-mile trips finds that basic trainers lacking speed and payload capacity impose frustrating limitations. Periodically examining actual flying patterns against capabilities and resources ensures that aviation engagement remains rational rather than persisting through inertia with equipment and training poorly matched to realistic missions.

Personal minimums establish operational boundaries that reflect individual comfort levels, skill proficiency, and risk tolerance rather than simply adhering to regulatory limits applicable to all pilots regardless of experience or capability. The Federal Aviation Regulations specify minimum visibility, cloud clearances, and aircraft equipment requirements for various operations. Still, these regulatory floors assume competent pilots operating at skill levels appropriate for the certificates and ratings they hold. Newly certificated pilots usually lack the experience to operate safely at regulatory minimums, particularly in marginal weather conditions, where regulation-compliant flight remains legal but can be dangerous for pilots without substantial experience managing challenging situations. Developing personal minimums requires honest self-assessment about capabilities, willingness to accept that initial limitations need not apply permanently, and discipline to maintain boundaries even when external pressures encourage exceeding them. A newly certificated pilot might reasonably establish personal minimums requiring five-mile visibility and three-thousand-foot cloud ceilings for cross-country flight, well above the three-mile visibility and standard cloud clearances that regulations permit for visual operations below ten thousand feet. These generous margins accommodate the additional workload that navigation, communication, and traffic avoidance impose on pilots who are still building experience as they integrate multiple tasks simultaneously. As experience accumulates and capabilities grow, personal minimums can relax toward regulatory limits, though even highly experienced pilots often maintain weather margins exceeding legal requirements because they recognize that regulatory minimums represent worst-case conditions acceptable for emergencies rather than standards for routine operations. Personal minimums extend beyond weather to encompass fuel reserves, fatigue levels, passenger pressures, time constraints, and countless other factors that influence flight safety. The discipline to honor these self-imposed boundaries even when circumstances tempt violations, the destination visible across a weather system that personal minimums preclude flying through, the passengers disappointed by cancellations, the business meetings threatened by weather delays, separates pilots who survive long enough to accumulate wisdom from those who become accident statistics illustrating why personal minimums exist and merit respect regardless of inconveniences their enforcement imposes.

Community involvement transforms aviation from a solitary pursuit into a shared passion that enriches both personal experience and broader aviation culture. Airports function as communities where regular presence and active participation create relationships that enhance flying enjoyment while contributing to aviation's continuation across generations. Attending airport board meetings, volunteering for maintenance days, supporting youth aviation programs, and participating in fly-ins and social events establishes identity as a community member rather than merely an airport user extracting value without contributing to communal welfare. These connections provide practical benefits, including learning about fuel price changes, runway closures, and local procedures before they create surprises; gaining recommendations for mechanics, instructors, or aviation resources; and accessing the collective knowledge of any active airport community. Beyond pragmatic advantages, community engagement satisfies social needs that solitary flying cannot address, creating friendships bonded by a shared passion for aviation and a mutual understanding of the commitment required to maintain flying privileges. The newly certificated pilot who isolates themselves, arriving only for scheduled flights and departing immediately afterward, misses opportunities to develop a sense of belonging that sustains aviation engagement amid inevitable challenges and frustrations. Young Eagles programs, aviation career days at schools, and similar outreach initiatives allow pilots to share their passion while inspiring the next generation of aviators. These mentorship activities provide perspectives on how privileged and remarkable aviation access truly is, combating the complacency that treats flight as a routine commodity rather than an extraordinary capability that previous generations could barely imagine and that much of the current global population cannot access. The time invested in community building returns dividends over decades of flying, creating support networks that weather financial challenges, help overcome skill plateaus or confidence crises, and celebrate milestones that non-aviation friends cannot fully appreciate.

The license earned through dedicated training and successful checkride completion represents authorization for a lifetime of flight, but that lifetime unfolds not automatically but through conscious choices about priorities, resource allocation, and ongoing commitment to skill development and safety consciousness. The certificate never expires, but without continuous engagement, the privileges it conveys become theoretical rather than practical, words on paper rather than lived reality. Statistics reveal that substantial percentages of certificated pilots become inactive within five years, their flying dreams deferred indefinitely or abandoned entirely as life circumstances shift, and aviation loses the priority that sustained it through certification. Avoiding this outcome requires treating aviation not as an accomplished goal but as an ongoing relationship that demands attention, resources, and dedication over years and decades. The most successful long-term pilots integrate flying into the fabric of life rather than treating it as a separate activity competing with other priorities. They find ways to combine aviation with different interests, such as flying to hiking trailheads, photographing landscapes from aerial perspectives, volunteering their aircraft and pilot services for charitable missions, or sharing flight experiences with family and friends. They build financial models that accommodate aviation expenses through dedicated budgets, protecting flying from competition with discretionary spending that might otherwise consume resources. They cultivate relationships with other pilots who reinforce commitment through social pressure and mutual support, making decisions about whether to fly or cancel individual trips within community contexts where others know about plans and outcomes. They pursue continuous learning through advanced ratings, specialized endorsements, safety seminars, and independent study, which prevents knowledge stagnation and skill decay. They approach each flight with the seriousness it deserves, recognizing that aviation's margin for error remains thin despite technological advances and safety improvements that make modern flying statistically safer than previous generations experienced. The newly certificated pilot standing at this threshold possesses something precious and hard-won: authorization to explore Earth's atmosphere with freedom and perspective denied to all but a tiny fraction of humanity. Whether that privilege extends across decades of rewarding flying or fades into a nostalgic memory of accomplishment not sustained depends entirely on decisions made during the months and years following checkride success —choices about priorities, commitments, and the determination to make skyward dreams not merely past achievements but a continuing reality.

Ready for Takeoff? Here's How to Start

If you've made it this far, one thing's clear:
You're not just curious about flying. You're seriously considering it.

So, here's your next step—not five steps, not a checklist a mile long—just **one decision** to get your journey off the ground.

Book a Discovery Flight

This is the aviation world's open door.

A **discovery flight** is your chance to sit in the left seat—with a certified instructor beside you—and actually fly. You'll handle the controls. You'll feel the plane respond. You'll taxi, take off, and maybe even do gentle turns or climbs.
No commitment. No test. Just a taste.

Look up local flight schools or flying clubs in your area. Search "discovery flight near me" and make the call. It usually costs around $100–$200. Cheaper than a new smartphone—and way more life-changing.

What to Expect Next

Once you've taken that flight, here's what the path usually looks like:

1. **Get a Medical Certificate (3rd Class FAA for PPL)**
2. **Start Ground School** (online or in-person theory training)
3. **Begin Flight Lessons** (dual instruction with a CFI)
4. **Solo Flight** (after endorsement)
5. **Written Exam**
6. **Checkride (Oral + Flight Test)**
7. **Get Your PPL!**

But don't worry about all that now. The map is there when you're ready. Your only mission today?

Get in the air once.
Feel what it's like.
Let that answer everything else.

Final Words

You're not just learning to fly an aircraft.

You're learning to fly **you**.

So, here's the call:

Find a school.
Book the flight.
Take the left seat.

The sky isn't just above you—it's ahead of you.

Reference:

Chapter	Topic / Assertion	Citation
Chapter 1: The Decision to Fly	Private pilot training costs and duration	Aircraft Owners and Pilots Association (AOPA). (2023). Learn to Fly Overview. https://www.aopa.org/training-and-safety/learn-to-fly
	Medical certification classes and process	Federal Aviation Administration. Guide for Aviation Medical Examiners. https://www.faa.gov/about/office_org/headquarters_offices/avs/offices/aam/ame/guide
	Student demographics and learning ability	FAA. Pilot's Handbook of Aeronautical Knowledge (FAA-H-8083-25C). https://www.faa.gov
	Instructor-student relationship, flight school selection	FAA. Aviation Instructor's Handbook (FAA-H-8083-9B). https://www.faa.gov
Chapter 2: The Language of the Skies	Aviation radio phraseology and phonetics	International Civil Aviation Organization (ICAO). (2023). Manual of Radiotelephony (Doc 9432). https://www.icao.int
	Readbacks, standard communication structure	FAA. Airplane Flying Handbook (FAA-H-8083-3C), Ch. 14. https://www.faa.gov
	CTAF and uncontrolled airport communications	FAA. Advisory Circular 90-66C – Non-Towered Airport Flight Operations. https://www.faa.gov/documentLibrary/media/Advisory_Circular/AC_90-66C.pdf

	Emergency comms (Mayday, PAN-PAN, squawk codes)	FAA. Airplane Flying Handbook (FAA-H-8083-3C), Ch. 17. https://www.faa.gov
Chapter 3: Ground School	Core private pilot knowledge areas	FAA. Private Pilot Airman Certification Standards (FAA-S-ACS-6B). https://www.faa.gov
	Aerodynamics, weather, and navigation principles	FAA. Pilot's Handbook of Aeronautical Knowledge (FAA-H-8083-25C). https://www.faa.gov
	Weather interpretation (METARs, TAFs, icing)	FAA. Aviation Weather Handbook (FAA-H-8083-28). https://www.faa.gov
	Decision-making, human factors in aviation	FAA. Risk Management Handbook (FAA-H-8083-2A). https://www.faa.gov
	Testing: knowledge exams, oral tests	FAA. Knowledge Testing Guide – Private Pilot Airplane (FAA-G-8082-17). https://www.faa.gov/training_testing/testing
Chapter 4: First Solo Flight	Solo endorsement and legal prerequisites	FAA. 14 CFR §61.87 – Solo Requirements for Student Pilots. https://www.ecfr.gov/current/title-14/chapter-I/subchapter-D/part-61
	Emotional and psychological prep for soloing	FAA. Aviation Instructor's Handbook (FAA-H-8083-9B), Ch. 8: Human Behavior. https://www.faa.gov
	Changes in aircraft performance when solo	FAA. Airplane Flying Handbook (FAA-H-8083-3C). https://www.faa.gov
Chapter 5: Aeronautical Decision-Making / Risk & Judgment	ADM process, 3-P model, human factors in accidents	Federal Aviation Administration. Aeronautical Decision Making (PDF). (FAA)

	Risk management as a decision-making aid	FAA. Risk Management Handbook (FAA-H-8083-2A) (FAA)
	Relationship of human error to accidents	FAA (2017). "Aeronautical Decision-Making: A Basic Staple." (FAA Safety)
Chapter 6: Emergencies, Failures & Abnormal Procedures	Emergency operations guidance	FAA. Airplane Flying Handbook (FAA-H-8083-3C), Chapter 17: Emergency Operations
	Radio failure, emergency communication standards	FAA. AIM / Advisory Circular 90 series / AIM chapters on communications
Chapter 7: Cross-Country & Advanced Navigation	Flight planning, navigation techniques, risk assessment	FAA. Flight Planning Guide for General Aviation (or related FAA planning publications)
	Performance analysis, fuel planning, margins	FAA. Pilot's Handbook of Aeronautical Knowledge (FAA-H-8083-25C)
Chapter 8: Weather, Icing & Advanced Meteorology	Weather theory, freezing conditions, icing risk	FAA. Aviation Weather Handbook (FAA-H-8083-28)
	PIREPs, TAF, METAR decoding	National Weather Service. Aviation Weather Services Guide
Chapter 9: Night, IFR, or Transitioning Conditions	Night operations, human limitations, night illusions	FAA. Instrument Flying Handbook / Airplane Flying Handbook (night chapters)
	Instrument procedures, IFR basics	FAA. Instrument Procedures Handbook (FAA-H-8083-16B)

Chapter 10: Single-Pilot Resource Management & Workload	SRM, workload management, and CRM applied to solo pilots	FAA. Risk Management Handbook, especially chapters on SRM/CRM (BigCommerce)
	Use of automation, managing multiple tasks	FAA. Aviation Instructor's Handbook (FAA-H-8083-9B), chapter on risk/instructor methods (ETL Aviation)
Chapter 11: Human Factors, Fatigue, Stress & Error Prevention	Human factors, error models, SHELL, HFACS, Dirty Dozen	"Dirty Dozen" list from FAA Safety (common human factors causes) (FAA Safety) HFACS / human factors classification system (Wikipedia) SHELL model overview (Wikipedia)
	Fatigue regulation, mental workload	FAA. Risk Management Handbook sections on personal risk (IMSAFE) (FAA)
Chapter 12: Checkride Preparation, Confidence & Lifelong Learning	ACS, knowledge test format, oral exam prep	FAA. Private Pilot Airplane Knowledge Testing Guide (FAA-G-8082-17)
	Continuing training, proficiency, and safety culture	FAA Safety Team human factors training modules (FAA Safety)

About The Author

Quinn Hartley grew up with eyes fixed on the sky and a restless curiosity about what it would take to leave the ground. Long before earning a pilot's license, Hartley was already chasing altitude in other forms — testing limits, questioning rules, and studying what gives people the courage to rise when everything around them insists on gravity. A lifelong adventurer and writer, Hartley has spent years exploring how the disciplines of flight—precision, awareness, adaptability—mirror the skills we need to navigate modern life.

In *The Book On Taking Flight*, Hartley brings together lessons learned in the cockpit with insights from psychology, performance science, and philosophy. The result isn't just a manual on aviation—it's a meditation on freedom, risk, and focus in an era that feels increasingly out of control. Hartley writes for those grounded not by fear but by uncertainty, showing how the principles of flight—lift, drag, thrust, and balance—can serve as a blueprint for reclaiming control and rediscovering purpose.

When not writing or flying, Hartley can often be found studying weather charts, rebuilding old gear, or helping others take their own first flights—whether that means a literal takeoff or a leap into something entirely new.

About The Publisher

Welcome to The Book On Publishing

At The Book On Publishing, we believe in rewriting the rules of learning. Whether you're chasing your next big idea, building a better life, or simply curious about what should have been taught in school, you've come to the right place.

We're a platform built for dreamers, doers, and lifelong learners, offering bold, practical books and tools that empower you to take charge of your journey. From real-world skills to mindset mastery, we publish the book on what matters.

No fluff. No lectures. Just what you need to know, delivered with clarity, purpose, and a spark of curiosity.

Start exploring. Start growing. Start writing your story.

Read more at https://thebookon.ca.

Acknowledgment of AI Assistance

Portions of this book were developed with the support of AI. While every word has been carefully reviewed and refined by the author, AI served as a valuable tool for brainstorming, editing, and structuring ideas. Its assistance helped accelerate the creative process and clarify complex topics.

www.ingramcontent.com/pod-product-compliance
Lightning Source LLC
Chambersburg PA
CBHW071743120626
46550CB00002B/638

9781997909392